GARLAND STUDIES ON

INDUSTRIAL PRODUCTIVITY

T0330925

edited by

STUART BRUCHEY
ALLAN NEVINS PROFESSOR EMERITUS
COLUMBIA UNIVERSITY

LINKING EMPLOYEE SATISFACTION TO BUSINESS RESULTS

PAULA S. TOPOLOSKY

Routledge
Taylor & Francis Group

LONDON AND NEW YORK

First published 2000 by Garland Publishing, Inc.

2 Park Square, Milton Park, Abingdon, Oxon OX14 4RN
711 Third Avenue, New York, NY 10017, USA

Routledge is an imprint of the Taylor & Francis Group, an informa business

First issued in paperback 2016

Library of Congress Cataloging-in-Publication Data is available from the Library of
Congress.

Topolosky, Paula S.
    Linking employee satisfaction to business results / Paula S. Topolosky
    p. cm. — (Garland studies on industrial productivity)
    Includes bibliographic references.
    ISBN 0-8153-3487-7 (alk. paper)
    1. Job satisfaction.   2. Job satisfaction—United States—Case studies.
3. Employee motivation—United States—Case studies.   I. Title.   II. Series.
    HF5549.5.J63T585   1999
    658.3'14—dc21   99-30495
    ISBN 978-0-8153-3487-3 (hbk)   CIP
    ISBN 978-1-138-99545-1 (pbk)

Contents

List of Tables

Preface

Business leaders are expected to make decisions that quickly and positively impact bottom line results. Whether intentional or unintentional, these decisions also impact employee satisfaction. Using data from a Fortune 100 Company, this historical study assessed trends in employee satisfaction over a six-year period and identified the relationships between thirty employee satisfaction variables and both corporate and business unit financial results. In this study, personal development, involvement and participation, use of skills and abilities, promotion practices, and opportunities for a better job were most positively correlated to Company financial results. Satisfaction with corporate change strategies, direction of the Company, employee benefits, balance between work and personal life, input to decisions, job security, and realizing personal benefits from attaining organizational goals were most negatively correlated with Company financial results.

LINKING
EMPLOYEE SATISFACTION
TO BUSINESS RESULTS

CHAPTER 1

Introduction

CENTRAL THEME

"Perhaps the greatest competitive challenge companies face is adjusting to—indeed, embracing—nonstop change" (Ulrich, 1998, p. 127). In business, "a rapidly changing economic environment characterized by such phenomena as the globalization and deregulation of markets, changing customer and investor demands, and ever-increasing product-market competition, has become the norm. . . . To compete, [business leaders] must continually improve their performance by reducing costs, innovating products and processes, and improving quality, productivity, and speed to market" (Becker & Gerhart, 1996, p. 779). In response to the competitive pressures, many leaders have experimented with, and continue to grasp at, a variety of improvement and change strategies to increase shareholder value and to gain a sustainable competitive advantage in the global market place. Both traditional techniques, such as pricing and product differentiation, as well as non-traditional methods, such as downsizing, re-engineering, and outsourcing, have been implemented in attempts to quickly and positively impact financial bottom lines (*The Conference Board*, 1993). However, in many firms, these attempts to compete have neither reaped the expected economic benefits, such as lower operating expenses, higher profits, increased rates of return on investments or improved stock prices, nor the organizational benefits, such as lower overhead costs, improved communications, greater entrepreneurship, or increases in productivity (Cascio, 1993, p. 95). Instead, "despite billions spent on process improvement and reorganization, workplaces are filled with fear, distrust, and paranoia" (Willingham,

1997, p. 1). Ironically, as employees were displaced by many of the business improvement strategies, and as other competitive strategies proved less successful, business leaders discovered that people are a unique source of competitive advantage (Pfeffer, 1994). In 1986, Schuster wrote that "it appears that increased attention to employees is going to have a major impact on business during the next two decades. Companies that begin to manage their human resources effectively to harness the untapped potential for commitment to the goals of the organization will forge ahead, while others will find they are unable to remain competitive" (p. 166).

This study focused on employee satisfaction as one measure of the effectiveness of managing human resources. Over twenty years ago, Locke (1976) estimated that more than 3,350 studies of employee satisfaction already existed in the research literature. By the volume of research, it would seem that knowledge of employee satisfaction is of some interest to industrial and organizational psychologists. But why should business leaders be concerned with employee satisfaction? Some might agree that satisfying employees makes moral and ethical sense. But does it make economic sense?

Using data from a Fortune 100 Company, this historical study assessed trends in employee satisfaction over a six-year period and identified the relationship between employee satisfaction and both corporate and business unit financial results. Though causality cannot be implied by the correlational design of this study, knowledge of the trends and relational outcomes might prove helpful to business leaders and Human Resource (HR) professionals in the identification and prioritization of work environment improvement initiatives that are better aligned with strategic business objectives.

STATEMENT OF THE PROBLEM

Is there a significant relationship between employee satisfaction and business results? Leaders are becoming aware that "people issues are business issues" (Schuler, 1990, p. 49). In her research investigating the links between employee satisfaction and organizational performance, Ostroff (1992) wrote that "it has been proposed that satisfaction and the happiness of personnel heighten organizational effectiveness. . . . Organizations that alienate workers through their practices will be less effective and efficient" (p. 964). This concept is not new. Past studies, including those of Etzioni (1964), Likert (1961), and McGregor, (1960), have implied that satisfied workers are productive workers. Ostroff (1992) noted that these theorists claimed that "organizational productivity is achieved through employee satisfaction and attention to workers' physical and emotional needs. . . . Whether or not an employee will give his or her services·wholeheartedly to the organization and produce up to potential depends, in large part, on the way the worker feels about the job, fellow workers, and supervisors" (p. 964).

In 1996, Jones noted that "today's managers recognize that they cannot achieve their key business objectives without the focus and commitment of the entire workforce. At the same time, however, they know that employees are more disillusioned than at any time in recent history with their companies' commitment for the long term" (p. 22). Denton (1991, p. 45) observed that there was evidence of a growing disenchantment and dissatisfaction in the workforce, even within organizations many had thought of as well run.

It is becoming clear to many corporations that to survive in the market place, business leaders must manage their human resources differently if they are to compete successfully (Beer, Lawrence, Mills, Spector, and Walton, 1984, p. vii). However, with all of the intense competitive pressures, organizations cannot afford to support improvement initiatives that are not obviously contributing to the strategic goals and success of the enterprise (Fitz-enz, 1994). Though leaders prefer to select and implement human resource improvement initiatives that would have the largest positive impact on financial and organizational results, there is currently limited relational research data available with which to make informed decisions.

PURPOSE OF THE STUDY

By investigating the relationship between employee satisfaction and financial results, this study attempted to provide research data to enhance leadership decisions to invest in human resource improvement initiatives that support business strategies.

In 1984, Beer et al wrote, "If [business leaders] are to determine what human resource policies and practices their firm should employ, they need some way to assess the appropriateness or effectiveness of those policies" (p. 15). One way to obtain feedback on the effectiveness of human resource initiatives is to ask employees directly. Snetsinger and Pellet (1996) wrote that "employee research provides essential information to propel improvement processes. . . . Acting on the voice of the em-

ployee is a key component in many successful organizational strategies"
(p. 13). Employee attitude surveys are important for organizations look-
ing to improve communications, to evaluate the impact of policies and
programs, to monitor reactions to change, to assess business strategy,
and to diagnose the reasons for organizational problems. A survey conducted for *Personnel Journal* by the Gallup Organization found that of
the 429 Human Resource directors surveyed, 1) 93% believe employee
research can be useful; 2) 70% of firms of all sizes report that they have
been involved in an employee attitude survey at least once during the
past 10 years; and, 3) 69% of companies say they are likely to conduct
another survey (Gallup, 1988, p. 42). However, despite the high usage
rates, Shull (1995) perceived surveys to have a poor return on investment
because few companies used survey information for decisions or action
planning, much less change (p. 138). In his book, *Integrating the Individual and the Organization*, Argyris (1995) supported the use of employee
data for organizational change when he noted that attempts to assess and
improve employee satisfaction are not just about keeping people happy.
He wrote that the goal of most organizations should be to foster compe-
tent, committed, self-responsible, fully functioning individuals in order
to ensure active, viable, and vital organizations (p. 4). Outcomes of this
study might help business leaders target improvements in work environments that can be mutually rewarding to both people and financial bottom lines.

NEED FOR THE STUDY

Three areas of need were identified for this study. These were the limited
amount of data from empirical studies linking systems of HR activities
and employee satisfaction to firm performance, methodological limita-
tions of past studies, and the demand within organizations for Human
Resources to provide evidence that would increase its value and capacity
to contribute to the success of business strategies. Huselid (1995, p. 636)
wrote:

> There is a growing consensus that organizational Human Resource
> policies can, if properly configured, provide a direct and economi-
> cally significant contribution to firm performance. The presumption is
> that more effective systems of HRM [Human Resource Management]
> practices, which simultaneously exploit the potential for complemen-
> tarities [alignments] or synergies among such practices and help to

implement a firm's competitive strategy, are sources of sustained competitive advantage. Unfortunately, very little empirical evidence supports such a belief. What empirical work does exist has largely focused on individual HRM practices to the exclusion of overall HRM systems.

MacDuffie (1995) observed that "despite claims that innovative human resource (HR) practices can boost firm-level performance . . . few studies have been able to confirm this relationship empirically, and still fewer have systematically described the conditions under which it [the relationship] will be the strongest" (p. 197). Becker and Gerhart (1996) noted the importance of getting a better understanding of the role of human resource decisions in creating and sustaining organizational performance and competitive advantage. They wrote, "Given the importance and complexities of the issue, the work that has been done is relatively small, and most of the key questions are sorely in need of further attention. . . . HR systems represent a largely untapped opportunity to improve firm performance" (p. 780). The authors suggested that "future work on the strategic perspective must elaborate on the black box between a firm's HR systems and the firm's bottom line" (p. 793). They observed that none of the past studies used business unit-level outcomes that indicated the difficulty of measuring performance at this level. Becker and Gerhart identified a need to fill in the gap at the business-unit level and to pay attention not only to traditional financial outcomes, but also to intermediate and process-related criteria that describe how financial results are achieved. They noted that past efforts suffered from method bias that occurred when one respondent was asked to provide information on both HR performance and firm performance. According to Becker and Gerhart, "Future research would benefit from the use of multiple raters from each organization, business unit, or facility [site] studied, particularly where subjectivity or judgment is required" (p. 795). The authors cited a need to hasten the development of a cumulative body of knowledge to provide a new strategic lever to senior management (p. 797).

Dewey and Hawk (1996) pointed out that "it is a truth of organizational life that HR has typically not been a player in the development of business strategies. . . . One reason is that HR professionals often lack a consistent business-based context for their work" (p. 30). Human Resources must increase business acumen and adopt measures of effectiveness that are aligned with business strategies. Ulrich, Losey, and Lake

(1997) suggested that the measure of HR effectiveness will not just be how well data on employee satisfaction is collected but on the commitment to improve people processes based on the results and on the ability to link improvement efforts to business strategies and results. Schuster (1986, p. 156) recommended that one way for HR to demonstrate business value was to link employee data to business outcomes. He suggested that

> Once a climate survey process has been in operation for several years, it is advantageous to make regular determinations of the correlation between changes in the measures of organizational climate and changes in the measures of organizational performance. This process can then serve as a control mechanism to assure that the organizational change strategy is having the intended payoff in terms of profitability and other long-term hard measures of performance. . . . The simplest way to measure the relationship is to determine the linear coefficient of correlation over a series of years between the numerical data representing the organizational climate and the numerical data representing the hard performance measures that have been selected . [by the organization].

RESEARCH QUESTIONS

This study was designed to address the following questions:

1. What is the relationship between employee satisfaction variables and seven business unit financial metrics: sales, growth, after-tax operating income, return on net assets, controllable cash flow, fixed cost productivity, and shareholder value added?
2. What is the relationship between employee satisfaction variables and nine corporate financial metrics: US sales, US earnings, US after-tax operating income, corporate sales, corporate earnings, corporate return on shareholder investment, earnings per share of common stock, dividends per share, and year-end stock market price?
3. Which employee satisfaction variables demonstrate the greatest and the least point estimates with respect to variability during the period of the study?

DEFINITION OF TERMS

The following are descriptions of terms that were used in this dissertation. Financial definitions, unless otherwise noted, were cited from an internal Company document, "Financial Metrics Definitions, 1996 Business Unit Performance Reporting".

After-tax Operating Income (ATOI). ATOI represents the "bottom line" for business unit earnings. ATOI is defined as total revenue (sales and transfers plus other income) less variable and fixed costs, net of taxes. Underlying ATOI values were used in this study which excluded the impact of transactions qualifying for treatment as nonrecurring items.

Company. In this study, Company, with a capital "C", refers to the Fortune 100 company targeted in this research.

Controllable Cash Flow. This term reflects the cash flow from operations plus or minus capital expenditures, cash to and from affiliates, non-operating cash inflow, financing costs and nonrecurring items.

Earnings per Share (EPS). Within the Company, EPS is determined by dividing earnings on common stock by the average number of shares outstanding during the reporting period.

Employee Commitment. According to Meyer and Allen (1991), this term refers to the psychological attachment of workers to their workplaces.

Employee Satisfaction Research. The term refers to studies that are undertaken to describe and understand the subjective experiences of individuals in the workplace (Taber, 1991).

Fixed Cost Productivity. This term is a measure of the sales and transfers generated by each dollar of controllable fixed costs. This ratio will increase if sales and transfers increase at a rate greater than fixed costs.

Growth. Sales growth measures the change in sales and transfers dollars expressed as a percentage of sales and transfers dollars for the same period in the prior year.

Human Resources (HR). This term, with a capital "H", refers to a specific function or group within organizations that supports the activities of the business units through the design and implementation of policies and procedures that enhance the effectiveness and efficiency of the management of employees.

Return on Net Assets (RONA). This term is a measure of the earnings or return on operating net assets employed by the Company. These assets include direct permanent investment, net working capital, and other indirect investments such as office buildings, and research facilities.

Return on Shareholder Investment. Data used for this study reflected the return on investors' capital. This term is a measure of the earnings available to meet all obligations to service investors' capital. Earnings represent net income before after-tax interest expense. Investors' capital includes short and long term borrowings.

Sales. Sales refer to all amounts billed for commercial finished product furnished and services rendered during the period to customers and affiliated companies in the ordinary course of business. For the purpose of this study, sales excludes transfers, which represent materials manufactured or purchased by one business unit to another for consumption or resale.

Shareholder Value Added (SVA). SVA measures the economic profit or value added by a business after recognizing the cost of capital related to the investment in operating net assets employed by the businesses. It is calculated by subtracting a capital charge from business operating earnings.

Strategic Business Unit (SBU). Within the Company targeted in this study, this term is used to identify a discrete group or subset of the total Company that includes all of the resources necessary to make, buy, and deliver products and services to specific markets or industries.

Sustainable Competitive Advantage. Pfeffer (1994) defined a sustainable competitive advantage as something that distinguishes a company from competitors, provides positive economic benefits, and is not readily duplicated.

CHAPTER REVIEW

This chapter has presented the central theme, statement of the problem, purpose of the study, need for the study, and research questions. In Chapter 2, the literature review discusses related research. It is organized into employee satisfaction surveys, organizational health, organizational wealth, and transformation and measurement of Human Resources. Chapter 3 details the design of this study and includes the research methodology and threats to validity, descriptions of the population and sample, and issues regarding instrumentation. Chapter 4 presents the results of the study in the form of correlational data to describe the relationship between employee satisfaction variables and business unit and corporate financial metrics. The chapter also includes results that describe the variability of employee satisfaction during the period of the study. In Chapter 5, the findings of the research are discussed. This chapter also includes statements on the generalizability, implications of the study, and recommendations for future studies.

CHAPTER 2

Review of the Literature

INCLUSION CRITERIA

This study used historical data from corporate employee attitude surveys and financial documents to investigate the relationship between levels of employee satisfaction and business results. Related research from the fields of industrial psychology, human resources, management and leadership, and business were used as the primary sources of information for this literature review.

The literature included in this review was organized into four sections; 1) *Employee Attitude Surveys*, which includes historical views of work, the relationship between work and life satisfaction, and examples of employee satisfaction research; 2) *Organizational Health*, which presents different visions of a healthy organization and the potential impact of a healthy culture on employee satisfaction and organizational results; 3) *Organizational Wealth*, which describes various stakeholders' perceptions of success and identifies ways that theories about human asset management and intellectual capital might impact employee satisfaction; and, 4) *Transformation and Measurement of Human Resources*, which describes efforts to improve business results through improved processes for the strategic management of people.

HISTORICAL VIEWS OF WORK

"By the 1930s, employee attitude surveys were being frequently used in business to assess and document employee morale" (Schneider, Ashworth, Higgs, & Carr, 1996, p. 695). However, employee perspectives of and satisfaction with work were forming long before that time. In the bible, Ecclesiastes, Chapter 2: verses 22–23, it was written that "labor does not satisfy the soul. . . . What does a man get for all the toil and anxious striving with which he labors under the sun? All his days are work and pain and grief"(*Women's Devotional Bible*, 1995, p. 728). To the ancient Greeks, in whose society mechanical labor was done by slaves, "work brutalized the mind and made man unfit for the practice of virtue. It was a necessary evil which the elite, in their search for changeless vision, should avoid" (Mills, 1951, as cited in Best, 1973, p. 7). Even today, some synonyms for work include words like drudgery, slavery, toil, grind, exploit, fatigue, and pain (Sisson, 1969, p. 684). These images of work are not very pleasant pictures of where many adults spend most of their waking hours. Yet, they may have served as the starting point for many individuals' interpretations and expectations of work and consequent levels of satisfaction.

"There was a time when, for the vast majority, work was a matter of necessity. Questions about whether someone liked or disliked his job, until most recently, carried little weight. Work was simply a part of life that made voluntary choices outside the workplace possible" (Mindell & Gorden, 1981, p. 7). During the 1950s, 1960s, and 1970s , Gallup polls showed that "81 to 91 percent of all workers were satisfied" (U.S. Department of Labor, 1974 Research Monograph, as cited in Mindell & Gorden, 1981, p. 7). However, in 1975, Fuller wrote that "dramatic forces of change are at work in our society today. There are signs of crisis in almost every major institution. Many of these center around people— the desire of individuals for a higher quality of life in their everyday lives and on the job" (Soujanen, McDonald, Swallow & Soujanen, 1975, p. 205). Almost two decades ago, the Opinion Research Corporation warned that employee satisfaction was decreasing and that satisfaction would be a major challenge for management in the 1980s (Cooper, Foley, Kaplan & Morgan, 1979, p. 118).

RELATIONSHIP OF WORK AND LIFE SATISFACTION

In the book *The Future of Work*, F. E. Best (1973) stated that "today, as in the past, our relationship to work activity is a fundamental determinant of the way we live. Our relation to work has determined and influenced our status, the kind of food available to us, our ability to buy goods, our use of time and leisure, the nature of our family and sexual relations, the state of our mental health, and an endless host of other conditions" (p. 1). Levering (1988) suggested the importance of work when he wrote,

"Work is central to our lives. . . . It defines our role in society. It determines our level of income and hence our standard of living" (p. 267). Peter Drucker (1974) wrote, "To make a living is no longer enough. Work also has to make a life" (p. 179). The relationship between work and life satisfaction has been the subject of many studies. Using correlations from 34 studies, Tait, Baldwin, and Padgett (1989) estimated that the correlation between job satisfaction and life satisfaction was .44 (p. 504). Other researchers, including Rice, Near, and Hunt (1980), Schmitt and Mellon (1980), Rain, Lane, and Steiner (1991), Thompson, Kopelman, and Schriesheim (1992), Deiner, Larsen, and Griffin (1985), and Judge and Watanabe (1993) studied the relationship between satisfaction with work and life but have drawn various (and in some cases opposing) conclusions on the recursiveness between the two constructs (as cited in Tait, Baldwin, and Padgett, 1989). More recently, Lawler (1994) linked the interest in work and job satisfaction to the concerns in many countries with the quality of life. He wrote that "job satisfaction is one measure of the quality of life in organizations and is worth understanding and increasing even if it doesn't relate to performance. . . . What happens to people during the workday has profound effects both on the individual employee's life and on society as a whole" (p. 80).

EMPLOYEE SATISFACTION STUDIES

One of the earliest indicators that there might be business benefits in employee satisfaction with work resulted from the Hawthorne efficiency experiments at Western Electric. These studies demonstrated, much to the astonishment of the researchers Mayo, Roethlisberger, Whitehead, Dickson, and Homams (Roethlisberger & Dickson, 1943), that increases in productivity might be gained by simply paying attention to employees. "To a certain extent, the Hawthorne studies have set the pattern for many recent investigations of social phenomena in industry" (Herzberg, Mausner, Peterson, & Capwell, 1957, p. 152). In 1982, Peters and Waterman surveyed 1,300 major firms in America. Similar to the findings in the Hawthorne studies, one of the conclusions of their study was that significant relationships exist between attention to employees, productivity, and superior organizational results (p. 6).

Thurstone & Chave (1929) and Hoppock (1935) were among some of the earlier researchers who developed assessment tools to measure employee attitudes and job satisfaction. Since that time, many studies were launched that focused on different aspects of employee satisfaction.

Examples of studies that have been selected for inclusion in this review are related to the employee satisfaction variables chosen for this study. For easier referencing, past research and literature have been organized into four groups. The groups differ in the focus of the studies and research methodologies that become increasingly complex due to the increased number of possible interrelationships between variables. Group I cites some of the earlier work in the field that identified the elements of job satisfaction and the effect of *personal factors* such as age, gender, and experience of employees. Group II includes studies that investigated the impact of *social dynamics* on employee satisfaction and individual performance. This includes areas such as communication, participation, recognition, development, leadership, and commitment. Group III includes studies that researched relationships between employee satisfaction and *organizational processes*, such as compensation systems and high-performing or innovative work practices. Finally, studies that were included in Group IV reflect recent trends in employee satisfaction research. These studies begin to investigate the impact of employee satisfaction on *organizational performance.*

Group I: Personal Factors. Some of the earliest employee satisfaction studies focused on identifying the elements that constitute job satisfaction. Herzberg et al (1957) wrote that the term job satisfaction is multidimensional. They stated that "there can be satisfaction with the specific activities of the job; with the place and working conditions under which the job is performed; or with specific factors such as economic rewards, security, or social prestige" (p. 1). Extensive research on the dimensions of job satisfaction was conducted by Hackman and Oldham (1975, 1980). Drawing on the work of Turner and Lawrence (1965), they identified the dominant dimensions of a job as task variety, autonomy, feedback, identity, and significance (as cited in Griffin, 1991, p. 425). Since each job dimension had the potential to impact employee satisfaction, the research of Hackman and Oldham served as the springboard for many other studies on job satisfaction and work design. Several longitudinal field experiments were conducted which included research by Griffin (1983) and Opren (1979). These studies supported the construct that work or job redesign had a positive effect on employee levels of motivation, satisfaction, or both. However, the outcomes of these studies did not demonstrate any significant impact of work redesign on individual performance (Griffin, 1991, p. 426). Hulin, Roznowski, and Hachiya (1986) focused their research on other variables that might influence job satisfaction (as cited in Howard & Frink, 1996, p. 280). Specifically, their studies researched the impact of personal factors such as differences in age, gender, and experience, or tenure, on employee satisfaction and individual performance.

Research on the relationship between age and work satisfaction has shown that worker satisfaction varies directly with age and that older workers tend to be more satisfied with their jobs than younger workers (Mottaz, 1987). Some researchers have theorized that these results could be related to the reward-accommodation hypothesis of Gruenberg (1979) which proposed that older workers assign more importance to intrinsic than extrinsic work rewards. Studies by Rhodes (1983) and Kacmar and Ferris (1989) confirmed a generally positive linear relationship between age and job satisfaction (as cited in Howard & Frink, 1996, p. 281). Rhodes (1983) presented empirical evidence that suggested that "older workers actually have lower absenteeism, turnover, illness, and accident rates, higher job satisfaction and more positive work values than younger workers (as cited in McEvoy & Cascio, 1989, p. 11). McEvoy and Cascio (1989) reported on 96 independent studies that reviewed age to performance correlations. They concluded that age and job performance were unrelated but that performance was related to turnover (p. 14). Using data from 24 studies, they found that good performers are significantly less likely to leave an organization than are poor performers. The authors speculated that one possible explanation for the results may be due to levels of employee satisfaction. They noted in their study that the relationship of performance to satisfaction was generally positive and that satisfaction and intent to leave, or satisfaction and turnover, were generally related negatively (McEvoy & Cascio, 1987, p. 758).

Studies conducted by Pond and Geyer (1987) explored whether or not employee age influenced the relationship between perceived work alternatives and job satisfaction. "Their analyses revealed that a Perceived Work Alternative X [times] Employee Age interaction significantly predicted job satisfaction" (p. 552). The authors recommended additional research to address how employees of different ages and in different stages of their careers conceptualize perceived work alternatives and job satisfaction (p. 556).

Studies that evaluated the impact of gender on job satisfaction included research by Tait, Padgett, and Baldwin (1989). These researchers, following the procedure for meta-analysis proposed by Hunter, Schmidt and Jackson (1982), found that though there was no difference between correlations for men and women on job satisfaction after 1974, there was a large difference between these correlations before 1974. The authors speculated that the explanation for the disappearance of gender differences in the correlation studies over time might have been caused by demographic changes in the workforce, as well as the changing role for women at work (p. 505). However, Davis, who conducted studies in 1977, found that women were less likely to be satisfied with their jobs than men (as cited in Savery, 1996, p. 19). Studies by Mottaz (1987) concluded that, generally, levels of overall work satisfaction and the determinants of work satisfaction were similar for males and females regardless of occupational level. After a review of research by Herzberg et al (1957), Quinn, Staines, and McCollough (1974), Hulin and Smith (1964), and Sauser and York (1978), Neil and Snizek (1988) concluded that "differences in job satisfaction between men and women are thought to have been an artifact of variables other than gender" (p. 203).

Herzberg et al (1957) studied morale in groups of workers differing in length of service. Their studies, and those of Arnold (1951), Hull and Kolstad (1942), and McClusky and Strayer (1940) showed that "workers begin with high morale which drops during the first year of service and remains low for a number of years. As service increases, morale tends to go up. These findings undoubtedly are related to the changes in job satisfaction with age" (Herzberg et al, 1957, p. 13). Hulin, Roznowski, and Hachiya (1986, as cited in Judge and Watanabe, 1993, p. 942) hypothesized that an employee's frame of reference influenced how an employee perceives current outcomes and concluded that job tenure related negatively to job satisfaction. Katz (1978) implied that there might be a curvilinear relationship between experience and satisfaction that is influenced by the job. He noted that too many years in the same job will reduce motivation as challenge to master a new task declines. Katz also noted that insufficient time to master a task might prevent individuals from developing a sense of competence and a continued desire to achieve.

Group II: Social Dynamics. This group of studies focused on those processes of organizational life that effect relationships between group members and, as such, might impact levels of employee satisfaction.

"In the 1994 National Study of the Changing Workforce, conducted by the Families and Work Institute in New York City, 'open communication' was ranked highest by respondents who were asked to list items that they had considered to be very important in choosing their current jobs. Everyone wants to know what's going on, especially if it affects them" (as cited in Nelson, 1996, p. 66). Schneider and Bowen (1985) found that the "lack of effective communications will potentially lead to a decrease in role clarity, an increase in job tension, and a decrease in job satisfaction" (as cited in Rogers, Clow, & Kash, 1994, p. 14). Downs and Hazen (1977), using the Communication Satisfaction Questionnaire (CSQ), identified a strong positive relationship between communication and satisfaction dimensions. Research by Clampitt and Downs (1993) supported the construct that satisfaction with communication had an above average impact on productivity, but he noted the lack of generalizability of their findings because of the unique characteristics of organizations (p. 24).

Participation has been defined as a process in which influence is shared among individuals who are otherwise hierarchical unequals (Locke & Schweiger, 1979; Wagner & Gooding, 1987, as cited in Wagner, 1994, p. 312). Many studies investigated the relationship between participation, or employees' involvement in decisions that affect their work, and employee performance and satisfaction. In their book, *The Age of Participation*, authors McLagan and Nel (1995) identified some of the forces that are driving organizations to be more participative (p. 25). They also reviewed some of the costs of implementing and maintaining a participative work environment (p. 29) and possible payoffs, as evidenced by the positive impact on performance and satisfaction (p. 42). The authors referenced several studies by Kravetz (1988), Huselid (1995), Ichniowski and Shaw (1995), and MacDuffie (1995) to support their theories. These studies concluded that firms that engaged in participative practices, however they were identified by the organization, significantly outperformed companies that did not use such practices. Other research on participatory practices included studies by Coch and French (1948), Locke and Schweiger (1979), and Miller and Monge (1986). These researchers acknowledged a moderately positive relationship between participation and satisfaction. Some of the more frequently cited research involving employee participation and involvement was done by Lawler who related participation to productivity (1992), quality programs (Mohrman, Lawler & Ledford, 1996), and pay practices (1981, 1990). Lawler (1994) observed that it was the adoption or the incorporation of the practices into the organizational culture that most impacted performance and satisfaction results. The positive relationship between participation and satisfaction was supported in the review of studies conducted by Cotton, Vollrath, Froggatt, Lengnick-Hall, and Jennings (1988). However, a meta-analysis conducted by Wagner and Gooding (1987) and redone by Wagner (1994) suggested that "though the relationship between participation and satisfaction is slightly positive, the effect size is small enough to raise practical significance" (Wagner, 1994, p. 312).

McCoy (1992) defined recognition as "an after-the-fact display of appreciation for a contribution" (p. 42). "Numerous research studies, founded on basic psychological truths, prove that people who receive attention, recognition, and praise from others become more cooperative and hard working" (Ludeman, 1989, p. 5). According to International Survey Research (ISR), a company specializing in employee attitude surveys, " recognition for good performance is the third job priority for UK [United Kingdom] workers after being treated with fairness and respect and job security. Interestingly, while 70% of people say recognition is very important, just 37% are satisfied with the recognition they are getting" (Sydeain, 1995, p. 72). Nelson (1996) noted that "in a recent national survey conducted by Robert Half International, a staffing and recruitment firm located in Menlo Park, California, limited praise and recognition was ranked as the primary reason why employees leave their jobs today—ahead of compensation, limited authority, and personality conflicts" (p. 66).

"When readers of *Psychology Today* were asked which aspects about the job they found most satisfying, the first three rankings, in order of importance were: the chance to do something that makes you feel good about yourself as a person; the chance to accomplish something worthwhile, and the chance to learn new skills" (Ludeman, 1989, p. 48). However, because of a "new deal" in employee-employer relationships (Csoka, *The Conference Board*, 1996, p. 6), employees have discovered a need to re-define their expectations for personal growth at work. Bookbinder (1996) reported that "only 45% [of employees] believe they will have the opportunity to advance in the future. . . . Though they may not expect opportunities to advance in the traditional sense. . . . they do expect opportunities for development. They understand that lifetime employment is unrealistic and that they must contribute to the business to survive. Development is one of the necessary survival tools" (*The Conference Board*, 1996, p. 16). Milligan (1996) observed that "employees want professional development and training. . . . They want to know that companies will help them become marketable" (*The Conference Board*, 1996, p. 10).

In the report *Work in the 21st Century*, Daniel Yankelovich and John Innerwahr wrote that 17 percent of workers today work for self-development (as cited in Ludeman, 1989, p. 47). More than half (57%) of 1,344 business people surveyed from eight countries, said that they would advance further in their field if they had more education (*Priority Management Systems,* 1990, p. 10). Research by Bishop (1994) indicated that employer-provided training raised productivity by almost 16% (as cited in Black & Lynch, 1996, p. 263). A study conducted by the U.S. Department of Labor found that increasing the average educational level of employees in a manufacturing plant increased productivity by 8% (as cited in *Lakewood Reports,* 1996, p. 12). Gordon (1997, p. 41) provided additional examples of return on investments for training and development. He noted improvements in product defect rates, employee turnovers, company revenues, and revenue per employee. However, despite the potential to impact employee satisfaction and productivity gains, "most companies don't offer [workers] any training at all. Just 15,000 employers—a mere 0.5 percent of the total—account for 90 percent of the $30 billion spent on training annually" (Henkoff, 1993, p. 62, as cited in *The Conference Board,* 1993, p. 15).

Bookbinder (*The Conference Board,* 1996) wrote that "obviously, employees want fair pay, benefits, and a positive work environment, but they also want real leaders. A leader is a person who has a clear vision for the company, conveys confidence in the organization's strategic goals, and involves employees in processes. . . . They [leaders] must exhibit a full understanding of the economics of the business. They must communicate, provide development and training opportunities, and deal with performance problems fairly and quickly" (*The Conference Board,* 1996, p. 16). A study to determine responsibilities of leadership, conducted from 1983 to 1988 by the Opinion Research Corporation, surveyed 100,000 people from Fortune 500 companies. One conclusion was that confidence in upper management had declined remarkably (Denton, 1991, p. 45). Is there a correlation between leadership and employee satisfaction?

In 1985, Bass introduced the concept of "transformational leadership" which is a process where leaders attempt to inspire performance beyond basic compliance. Transformational leaders articulate and model a vision for the organization, stimulate new ideas from followers, demonstrate concern for individual development through support and recognition, and delegate responsibility to followers for job level decisions (Bass, 1985; Kouzes & Posner, 1988, as cited in Niehoff, Enz, & Grover, 1990, p. 338). Studies by Niehoff, Enz, and Grover (1990) assessed the relationship of transformational leadership characteristics to employee commitment, job satisfaction, and role ambiguity. Their studies found that these leadership actions were positively correlated with commitment and satisfaction and negatively correlated with role ambiguity (p. 344). These findings agreed with other research on leadership. For example, research conducted by Yukl (1994) concluded that there was a positive relationship between supportive leadership behaviors and employee attitudes. In a study to identify elements of excellent companies, Peters and Waterman (1982) demonstrated that productivity was improved as a result of leadership behaviors.

An area of research that has gained momentum recently is the relationship between employee satisfaction and commitment. Authors Jaffe, Scott, and Tobe (1994) wrote that "the demands on organizations today are so great that they cannot operate without high commitment from their employees" (p. xii). Organizational commitment was defined by McNeese-Smith (1996) as "the measure of strength of the employee's identification with, and involvement in, the goals and values of the organization" (p. 164). Mowday, Porter, and Steers (1982) defined organizational commitment as "strong belief in the organization's goals and values, a willingness to exert considerable effort on behalf of the organization, and a strong desire to remain a member of the organization (p. 82). Becker, Billings, Eveleth, and Gilbert (1996) defined employee commitment as a psychological attachment of workers to their workplaces. As such, Becker et al, cited empirical studies to support the constructs that employee commitment is positively related to job satisfaction (Bateman & Strasser, 1984; Mowday, Porter, & Steers, 1982), motivation (Mowday, Steers & Porter, 1979), and attendance (Mathieu & Zajac, 1990). The research of Clegg (1983) and Cotton and Tuttle (1986), that focused on employee loyalty and commitment, concluded that commitment was negatively related to absenteeism and turnover. Meyer and Allen (1991) and Ward and Davis (1995) referred to three forms of organizational commitment. These included affective commitment or the strength of an individual's identification with and involvement in a particular organization; continuance commitment or the recognition that one would loose benefits upon leaving; and, normative commitment or a willingness to remain in an organization because of agreement or alignment with cultural norms and values or a sense of moral obligation" (Ward & Davis, 1995, p. 35).

A lack of commitment, or a lack of loyalty, might be costly to organizations. Reichheld (1996) wrote, "On the average, U.S. corporations now lose half their customers in five years, half their employees in four, and half their investors in less than one. Disloyalty at current rates stunts corporate performance by 25-50%" (p. 1). Tett and Meyer (1993) cited studies by Bluedorn (1979), Clegg (1983), and Douherty, Bluedorn, and Keon (1985) and concluded that commitment and satisfaction are positively related to each other (p. 259). They also cited studies by Arnold and Feldman (1982), Bluedorn (1982), and Hollenbeck and Williams (1986) as support for the construct that satisfaction was negatively related to turnover and intent to leave, which they associated with levels of employee commitment.

In his book, *Competitive Advantage Through People*, Pfeffer (1994) wrote that commitment is reciprocal. He stated that "security of employment signals a long-standing commitment by the organization to its work force. Norms of reciprocity tend to guarantee that this commitment is repaid, but conversely, an employer that signals through word and deed that its employees are dispensable is not likely to generate much loyalty, commitment, or willingness to expend extra effort for the organization's benefit" (pp. 31–32). Job commitment was the subject of a study conducted in 1994 by Zimney for Cambridge Reports Research International. The study concluded that commitment or loyalty to the employing organization, defense of the organization, personal job involvement, existence of outside priorities, and personal investment in the job were factors that contributed most to levels of employee satisfaction (p. 9). Using a commitment erosion index, the study identified the following as factors that led to employee dissatisfaction and loss of employee commitment: promotion policies, wage equity, fairness of employee policies, and interpersonal skills of management (p. 16).

Vandenberg and Lance (1992) reviewed studies that investigated the recursiveness of job satisfaction and commitment. They cited studies that resulted in a variety of outcomes. For example, Bateman and Strasser (1984) concluded that organizational commitment drove job satisfaction. Marsh and Mannari (1977) and Williams and Hazer (1986) found satisfaction to be a precursor of commitment (as cited in Glisson & Durick, 1988). Farkas & Tetrick (1989), in a longitudinal analysis of the impact of satisfaction on turnover, identified a reciprocal relationship between job satisfaction and organizational commitment. Other studies by Lance (1991) concluded that there was no significant relationship between satisfaction and commitment.

Group III: Organizational Processes. Several recent studies have focused research on the impact of the interrelationship of organizational processes on employee satisfaction. These studies included a focus on compensation systems and high-performing work practices.

Berlet and Cravens (1991) wrote that "direct employee compensation represents a powerful tool for improving organizations. If used properly, employee pay systems can enhance job satisfaction and create high levels of motivation that translate into productivity improvement" (as cited in Phillips, 1996, p. 216). Compensation systems were created in the 1950s and 1960s because people felt pay practices were out of control (Wilson, 1995, p. 8). Fitz-enz (1995) wrote, "Pay may or may not be the most important issue on the minds of employees, but few issues are more sensitive" (p. 119). A compensation system might include such things as base pay and merit increases, as well as non-traditional pay plans involving a variety of bonus arrangements and incentive plans (Berlet & Cravens, 1991, as cited in Phillips, 1996, p. 216). The theoretical foundations upon which compensation strategies have been developed were a result of many scientists, primarily behavioral psychologists, who studied sources of employee motivation and satisfaction. Lawler (1994) cited several theories that were developed earlier and provided insight into the effectiveness of compensation systems. These included fulfillment theories, such as those of Schaffer (1953) and Vroom (1964); discrepancy theories which were based on research by Katzell (1964), Locke (1968, 1969), and Porter (1961); and, equity theory as described by Adams (1963) (as cited in Lawler, 1994, pp. 84-91).

Locke (1969) wrote that "satisfaction is determined by the simple difference between what the person wants and what he perceives he receives. The more his wants exceed what he receives, the greater his dissatisfaction" (as cited in Lawler, 1994, p. 85). "Much research shows that unless they are rewarded more highly, people who have high inputs tend to be the most dissatisfied" (Lawler, 1994, p. 179). Lawler (1981) wrote that "despite the enormous amount spent on wages, commissions, cost of living increases, bonuses, and stock options, many studies have shown that, in most organizations, 50 percent or more of employees are dissatisfied with pay. . . . There is a continual 'noise' level about its adequacy and equity" (as cited in Beer et al, 1984, p. 116). Fitz-enz (1995) noted that "people fundamentally ask themselves two questions about their pay. First, am I paid fairly? Is the amount of money I make appropriate for the effort and responsibility I put into the job? Second, does the ratio of my input to my outcome compare favorably with the same ratio for other workers in my company, locale, and industry?" (p. 118).

According to a 1983 survey designed to study the impact of compensation policies that was conducted by the Opinion Research Corporation, "a majority of employees come to work each day believing that their wages are unfair, that pay increases are unfair, and that any improvement in their performance is unlikely to result in better pay" (Schiemann, 1983, as cited in Beer et al. 1984, p. 116). In 1986, another survey conducted by the Opinion Research Corporation, using input from 108,000 employees, found that 43 percent of employees did not believe that good performance would lead to a pay increase (Ludeman, 1989, pp. 179–180). In a survey consisting of 845 respondees, conducted by Public Agenda Foundation, 45 percent of workers surveyed did not see a link between pay and performance (as cited in Denton, 1991, p. 46). Equity issues escalate when comparing compensation differences between workers and high level management. Drucker (1989) noted that one characteristic of a poorly performing organization is the fact that top executives are paid more than 130% of the compensation of the people in the next echelon (as cited in Denton, 1991, p. 46).

Pay and compensation studies included research that focused on the basis or criteria for reward distribution (Kerr, 1985); short versus long term emphasis (Rappaport, 1978); corporate versus division performance (Pitts, 1976); internal versus external equity (Miles & Snow, 1984); quantitative versus qualitative performance measures (Napier & Smith, 1987); structure and design of compensation packages (Gerhart & Milkovich, 1990); fixed pay versus incentives (Galbraith & Merrill, 1991; Slater, 1973); frequency of raises or bonuses (Hambrick & Snow, 1989); impact of organizational policies (Miles & Snow, 1984); open versus secret pay (Lawler, 1990); and, bureaucratic versus flexible pay policies (Weber & Rynes, 1981) (as cited in Gomez-Mejia, 1992, p. 382). Despite the volume of studies, Klaas and McClendon (1996), citing Boudreau (1988) and Gerhart and Milkovich (1990), commented on the lack of existing models for estimating the financial impact of various pay policies (p. 122). Both Gomez-Mejia (1992) and Lawler (1981) noted the limited empirical research on organizational performance consequences of a compensation strategy. Lawler (1981) wrote that "most of the research [on pay] is fragmented, noncumulative, and poorly designed. Most of the forty-nine studies [reviewed by Lawler] that have tried to determine how important pay is represents a great expenditure of effort that contributes virtually nothing to our understanding. By selectively using data from these studies, one can argue any position" (p. 59).

The term high-performing or innovative work practices has several meanings in the literature. For some practitioners, "it refers to employee involvement efforts such as work teams (Katz, Kochan, & Gobeille, 1983). For others, it means employee participation in the financial well-being of the company, such as profit sharing, employee stock ownership, or pay-for-performance. Still others have in mind flexible and broadly defined job assignments. . . . " (Ichniowski, Kochan, Levine, Olson, & Strauss, 1996, p. 300).

High-performing or innovative work practices, as described by Huselid (1995), includes comprehensive employee recruitment and selection procedures, incentive compensation and performance management systems, and extensive employee involvement and training (p. 635).

"Often the term is used synonymously to describe a work culture that departs from the traditional work system that is characterized by tightly defined jobs with associated rates of pay, clear lines of demarcation separating duties and rights of workers and supervisors, decision-making powers retained by management, and communication and conflicts channeled through formal chains of command and grievance procedures" (Ichniowski et al, p. 300). Among many positive outcomes, these practices can improve the knowledge, skills, and abilities of a firm's current and potential employees, increase their satisfaction and motivation, and enhance retention of quality employees in an organization (Jones & Wright, 1992; U.S. Department of Labor, 1993, as cited in Huselid, 1995, p. 635). The systems are attractive to employees who seek greater degrees of flexibility in work organization, cooperation between labor and management, and participation in decisions on the financial well-being of the company (Ichniowski et al, p. 300).

"More than 2,500 studies have been done to correlate financial returns with high performance work practices" (Garner, 1996, p. 58). From an organizational perspective, Huselid (1995) concluded that an increase in high performance work practices could increase a firm's market value by $18,614 per employee over five years and improve productivity, turnover, and cash flow up to 8% (p. 18). For an employee, high performing work practices or systems might provide opportunities for personal contribution, socialization, involvement, personal growth, and performance feedback, which have been identified by Lawler (1994) as elements of a highly satisfying organizational culture.

Group IV: Organizational Performance. Several studies focused on individual human resource practices and the impact on various aspects of firm performance. For example, Terpstra and Rozell (1993) found a significant and positive link between the use of formal selection procedures and firm profits. Bartel (1994) demonstrated a link between the adoption of training programs and firm financial performance and productivity growth. McEvoy and Cascio (1987) demonstrated that job enrichment interventions were moderately effective in reducing turnover. The use of performance appraisals (Borman, 1991) and aligning appraisals and compensation (Gerhart & Milkovich, 1990) were connected with increased firm profitability (as cited in Huselid, 1995, pp. 639-640).

In a 1992 study of 298 schools designed to evaluate school environment and school effectiveness, Ostroff (1992) observed that previous research has consistently shown little relationship between job satisfaction, job attitudes, and performance for individuals. She recommended that researchers look at organizational levels of performance and suggested that "it is likely that a study of satisfaction to performance at the organizational level would show that organizations that have more satisfied employees are more productive and profitable than organizations whose employees are less satisfied" (p. 963).

Several studies began to investigate the impact of multiple variables on organizational performance. For example, the effect of HR practices on productivity included studies by Cutcher-Gershenfeld (1991), Katz, Kochan, and Gobeille (1983), Katz, Kochan, and Keefe (1988), and Katz, Kochan, and Weber (1985). Other studies, which included research by Arnold and Feldman (1982) and Cotton and Tuttle (1986) concluded that perceptions of job security, the presence of a union, compensation level, job satisfaction, organizational tenure, demographic variables, such as age, gender, education, and number of dependents, and the expressed intention to search for another job were all predictive of employees leaving and associated organizational expenses (Huselid, 1995, p. 638).

As indicated earlier, research by Huselid (1995), based on a sample of 968 large and medium-sized firms in thirty-five U.S. industries, assessed the effect of high performance work practices on a firm's economic profits, employee turnover, and productivity, as measured in sales per employee. His research included many variables, such as industry differences, firm size, union coverage, sales growth, research and development intensity, and total assets of the firm (Zigarelli, 1996, p. 63). Studies by Huselid and Becker (1996) presented field data to confirm some of the earlier conclusions from utility analysis research that a one standard deviation increase in employee performance, measured in dollars, is approximately equivalent to 40 percent of salary per employee. These findings had strong financial implications, particularly for large companies. Huselid (1995) concluded that high performance work practices had an economically and statistically significant impact on both immediate employee outcomes (turnover and productivity) and short- and long-term measures of corporate financial performance. He found that an increase in the deployment of high performance work practices reduced turnover by 7 percent, increased sales per employee by more than $27,000 per year, and enhanced profitability by more than $4,000 per employee (Zigarelli, 1996, p. 63).

In 1995, MacDuffie used the concept of "bundles" of HR practices and found that internally consistent HR practices were associated with higher productivity and quality in 62 automotive assembly plants. Ichniowski, Shaw, and Prennushi (1993) used longitudinal data from 30 steel plants to assess the impact of cooperative and innovative HRM practices on organizational productivity. Using research from the steel industry, Arthur (1994), found that those sites that emphasized the development of employee commitment had lower turnover, labor costs, reduced scrap rates, and higher productivity. Delaney and Huselid (1996) found that the use of progressive management practices had a strong and negative influence on organizational turnover in the manufacturing sector. Kravetz (1988) and Schuster (1986) studied global human resource management practices on firm profits. Baird and Meshoulam (1988), Begin (1991), Cappelli and Singh (1992), Lengnick-Hall and Lengnick-Hall (1988), and Wright and McMahan (1992) examined the impact of "fit" on organizational performance. This concept referred to the consistency or adoption of practices by the organization, such as alignment with competitive business strategies.

ORGANIZATIONAL HEALTH

"Healthy people make healthy companies. And healthy companies are more likely, more often, and over a longer period of time, to make healthy profits and to have healthy returns on their investments" (Foreword by Autry, as cited in Rosen, 1991, p. vii). "A link exists between a healthy workplace and job satisfaction. Most of those who say their workplace is healthy also say they're extremely well satisfied with their job. Similarly, most of those who say their workplace is unhealthy report being dissatisfied with their job" (*Priority Management Systems*, 1990, p. 6). What does a healthy company or a healthy organization look like? How does organizational health influence employee satisfaction?

Many authors and researchers have offered their visions of the characteristics necessary for organizational health. "For some time, the measure of business organization effectiveness could be discussed in one word, profit" (Argyris, 1993, p. 3). Prompted by the studies of several psychologists, such as Maslow (1943), McGregor (1960), and McClelland (1987), organizational researchers began to consider the human side of work. "Originally, much of the research seemed to be stimulated by a desire to show that job satisfaction is important because it influences productivity" (Lawler, 1994, p. 80). Argyris (1995) proposed that the real issue of humanistic research was one of integrating the individual and the organization where "both have to give a little to profit from each other" (p. 3). Some cultures were already aware of the importance of the interdependency between the business and human sides of work. For example, to the Swedes, the word for business is "närings liv". Translated, this means nourishment for life (Foreword by Senge, as cited in DeGeus, 1997, p. xi). In the Swedish culture, therefore, a healthy business might be described as one that nourishes the physical, mental, and spiritual aspects of humans.

In his book, *The Healthy Company*, author Robert Rosen (1991) described a healthy organization as one where "people and practices combine and coordinate to produce exceptional performance. . . . where all within the organization possess and emanate a certain vitality and spirit" (p. 9). Rosen listed several outcomes of healthy companies. These included such things as healthy leaders, quality service, employee loyalty and commitment, creativity and innovation, job satisfaction, and business success (p. 10). He referenced several studies to support the concept that "healthy companies enhance the development of people and add value to the bottom line" (p. 12). Rosen cited research by Kravetz (1988), who found that companies with progressive people management styles had 64 percent higher annualized sales growth over a five year period and better profit margins than those without a people-oriented culture (pp. 12-13).

Maccoby (1995), in the book *Why Work*, visually depicted a healthy organization as one that balances economic value added (EVA), customer value added (CVA) and people value added (PVA) (p. 235). Levering (1988), who used the concept of a "great place to work" to identify satisfying work environments, stated that what is important about a healthy organization is that profits are not something to be achieved at the expense of people. "In a great workplace, it is possible to achieve business success while enriching the lives of the people who work there" (p. ix). He posited that "from an employee viewpoint, a great workplace is one in which you trust the people you work for, have pride in what you do, and enjoy the people you are working with" (p. 26). Levering identified that, based on earnings per share and stock appreciation, healthy companies were twice as profitable as the average for the Standard and Poor's 500 (p. 259). The concept of "balance" between financial and non-financial measures of success was referenced in the book entitled *The Balanced Scorecard.* Authors Kaplan and Norton (1996) recommended that the best way to evaluate the success of a business was to use financial, employee, and customer satisfaction metrics (p. 9).

On a surface level, there are some authors whose perspectives of healthy organizations might appear to be opposing concepts. For example, Kouzes and Posner (1988), Drucker (1989), and Yukl (1994) were a few authors, among many, who have espoused the importance of leadership to a healthy organization. Though leadership is acknowledged as a critical factor, others, such as Lawler (1994) and Kayser (1994) championed employee empowerment, involvement, and teamwork, or collaboration, within various parts of the organization. They provided empirical evidence of a positive influence of employee participation and involvement on satisfaction and financial results. According to Kayser (1994), "Collaboration is the pathway to competitive success for any organization. . . . Teamwork fulfills individual need for control over work as well as social needs which has a higher satisfaction level" (p. 16). Gertz and Baptista (1995) advocated growth as a source of individual satisfaction and organizational success. They cited a 1994 study of over 4,000 Americans, conducted by the Wyatt Company, that found that "only 57 percent of workers in downsizing companies were generally satisfied with their work, as opposed to 72 percent in growing companies" (p. 19). Tomasko (1996) wrote that "growing a business and growing a person have a lot in common" (p. 13). He noted that "growth has many financial rewards to offer, but it also provides the opportunity to forge a link between the material world of a business—products, money, and promotions—and the 'softer' needs of the human psyche. Being a part of something bigger than ourselves and building something that can outlast ourselves are important cravings. They offer a chance to grow personally, to forge new relationships, to acquire new talents, and to challenge old assumptions" (pp. 12-13). On the other hand, Womack and Jones (1996) advocated the benefits of "lean thinking", a concept of doing more with less. Though seemingly contradictory to Gertz and Baptista and Tomasko, these authors were focused on organizational health and success but, primarily, through the elimination of waste. "Lean thinking" philosophy, according to Womack and Jones, would make work more satisfying by providing immediate feedback on efforts to convert waste into value (p. 15). Aligned with lean thinking philoso-phies, Zoltners, Sinha, and Murphy (1997) recommended that organiza-tions emphasize selection, development, reward, and organization as processes to transform groups from "fat to fit" (p. 230). To these au-thors, a "fit firm upgrades its processes, adapts its culture, and grows its people" (p. 267).

In their book, *The Power of Alignment*, Labovitz and Rosansky (1997) wrote that "alignment", or the focus of organizational systems and processes on similar organizational goals and objectives, was the cure for "symptoms of ailing growth and profitability" (p. 51). According to these authors, alignment, or focusing on the "Main Thing", has en-abled organizations to "establish a climate and culture that results in breakthrough levels of employee satisfaction, customer loyalty, and fi-nancial return" (p. xiii). Health is derived from a sense of order and stay-ing centered and aligned. On the otherhand, Peters (1987), in his book *Thriving on Chaos*, recommended that "to match the accelerating rate of change in the environment, numerous innovation projects must be mounted" (p. 244). Hurst (1995) noted the importance of being able to handle the crises and challenges of rapid change for organizational sur-vival and renewal.

In addition to the differences in visions of healthy companies, the issue of causality has been a source of philosophical and research debate. Do healthy people cause healthy organizations? Or, do healthy organiza-tions (and successful businesses) lead to healthy people? Blanchard and Johnson (1983) posited that "people who feel good about themselves produce good results" (p. 19). Norman Vincent Peale wrote that people who produce good results feel good about themselves (as cited in Can-field & Miller, 1996, p. 62). Swanson and Holton (1997) wrote that "today, we understand that productive employees who are able to achieve excellence, while being treated fairly, will be satisfied employ-ees who in turn will continue to be productive" (p. 6). Ouchi (1981) sug-gested that "humanized working conditions not only increase productivity and profits to the company but also increase the self-esteem for employees" (p. 165). Irrespective of the difference in visions and causality issues, organizational health has been frequently related to the caliber of people in organizations. Despite the variety and volume of lit-erature, organizations appear to be struggling to attain health as evi-denced by some of the signs of "organizational illness".

Organizations, like people, have distinct personalities and, like peo-ple, sometimes get sick. When the organization's personality is sick, it infects the people within and around it. If allowed to go untreated, the illness can cause serious harm, even a complete breakdown (Cohen & Cohen, 1993, p. 1). "Complaining and job dissatisfaction become an insidious organizational disease and the work systems begin to break down. . . . Many people consider their jobs as something they have to do, a burden imposed from the outside, an effort that takes life away from the ledger of their existence" (Cohen & Cohen, 1993, p. 4). DeGeus (1997) and Senge (1990) cited learning disabilities, or the inability to adapt and evolve as the world changes, as other indicators of an unhealthy organization and sources of dissatisfaction. As with any diseased state, some ailments are obvious; others might be hidden. Whether overt or not, pathological conditions can lead to both personal and organizational losses. Rosen (1991) identified some of the consequences of unhealthy organizational cultures. These included outcomes such as poor morale, increased grievances, poor judgment, reduced productivity, and job dissatisfaction (p. 9).

Even the language in an unhealthy organization changes. For example, employees who remain in the downsized organizations are often referred to as "survivors" (Johansen & Swigart, 1994) or the "wounded" (Noer, 1995). Arie DeGeus (1997) wrote that "companies die prematurely because their managers focus on the economic activity of producing goods and services, and forget that their organizations' true nature is that of a community of humans" (p. 3). There are different degrees of ills in organizations. The impact of an unhealthy organization on employee satisfaction depends on both the importance of the condition as perceived by the employee, and the frequency, severity, and duration of the problems (Bridges, 1980, as cited in Woodward & Buchholz, 1987).

ORGANIZATIONAL WEALTH

In the book, *The New Organizational Wealth*, Sveiby (1997) wrote that "people are the only true agents in business. All assets and structures—whether tangible or intangible—are the result of human actions. All depend ultimately on people for their continued existence" (p. 8). Fitz-enz (1997) observed that "in the information or knowledge era, the most distinguishing asset of every institution is its people. . . . Cash, facilities, equipment, and material....are all inert. High returns on their investment are totally dependent on human actions. . . . No amount of capital will ever be enough to offset the absence of knowledgeable, motivated people" (pp. 6-7). The challenge within organizations is to ensure that systems and processes are aligned to support the concept that people are an organization's most important asset.

"Traditionally, management has tended to view labor in terms of supply and demand, with employees viewed as short-term expenses to be minimized at every opportunity" (Shonhiwa & Gilmore, 1996, p. 18). Caudron (1994) wrote that "yesterday, the company with access to the most capital or the latest technology had the best competitive advantage. Today, companies that offer products with the highest quality are the ones with a leg up on the competition. But the only things that will uphold a company's competitive advantage tomorrow is the caliber of people in the organization" (p. 54). "Human assets" is a term used to represent the combination of knowledge, skills, and reasoning abilities (KSAs) possessed by a work force. It is widely recognized that the quality of an organization's human assets is key to high performance and a competitive advantage in formal organizations (Carnevale, 1996, p. 5). Human asset management or human capital theories maintain that "people in an organization should be viewed and managed as a portfolio of assets—a cluster of valuable holdings represented by a credit balance in the accounting books" (Shoniwa & Gilmore, 1996, p. 17). Several authors, including Argyris (1995), Ulrich & Lake (1990), and Pfeffer (1994), have promoted a firm's human resources as the only source of competitive advantage since human experiences are unique and cannot be easily duplicated by competitors. Schneier (1997) stated that "while it is probably not always true, as some claim, that human resources are the only source of competitive advantage, human capital is clearly the crucial factor driving whatever the source of advantage might be" (p. 16).

Frequently, employees are not only not managed as assets, but are ignored by the organization. "With no opportunities for involvement, employees become an untapped asset within most companies. The Southern California Suburban Policy Institute conducted a survey among employees of small-to medium-sized companies in 1994. Over 86 percent of employees felt that they had little or no impact in the daily decision making of their companies. Slightly more than half believed they were actively discouraged from offering input. Not surprising, nearly 70 percent expressed job dissatisfaction" (Birchard, 1995, p. 6).

Recently, Canfield and Miller (1996, p. 1) wrote:

> The heart of the workplace has been broken. . . . People are dropping out of jobs at alarming rates—from long-held senate seats and secure positions on Wall Street to jobs at all levels in the corporate world. For

those of us who choose to see, we find that insecurity, fear, despair, resignation, and cynicism are all at an all-time high. . . . Employees have been told that they are unessential by government shutdowns, computerization, and the effects of greed-motivated downsizing. The message is profits come before people, and as a result the dreams of a better life have become the nightmares of disappointment for far too many people.

Winston Churchill once said, "The empires of the future are empires of the mind" (as cited in Allee, 1997, p. xi). Intellectual capital is another source of organizational wealth. It has been defined as "the sum of everything everybody in a company knows that gives it a competitive edge. . . . it is the knowledge of a workforce." (Stewart, 1997, pp. ix-x). Stewart (1997) wrote that "you would be hard pressed to find a single industry, a single company, a single organization of any kind, that has not become more information-intensive—dependent on knowledge as a source of what attracts customers and clients" (p. 18). "Nowadays it is appreciated that approximately sixty percent of the competitive advantage in organizations comes from advances in worker intelligence (Carnevale, 1996, p. 5).

The selection, growth, and retention of employees within an organization have been identified by several authors (Pinchot & Pinchot, 1996; Thurbin, 1995) as the keys to intellectual capital. Brooking (1997) wrote that "every time we lose an employee we lose a chunk of corporate memory. Despite the fact that the organization pays for people—their asset—by way of salary and investments in them by way of training. . . . the asset (the employee) is not owned by the organization" (p. 9). Processes for managing intellectual capital include the identification of the sources of tacit and explicit knowledge, creation and maintenance of the knowledge, development of systems for knowledge sharing, measurement of the value of the knowledge, systems for standardizing knowledge for easy retrieval, destruction of irrelevant data and establishment of control systems to continuously grow and retain knowledge within the system. For these processes to work, employees must be motivated to learn in order to continuously renew the bank of knowledge and skills (Thurbin, 1995, pp. 160-164), to collaborate and share, and be energized to use information both at work and in personal life. In addition, employees need to be valued and respected for diverse experiences, challenged by their work, empowered by their leadership, acknowledged for their efforts, and committed and satisfied with their work environment (Pinchot & Pinchot, 1995).

Traditionally, to ensure longevity, business leaders were responsible for satisfying the shareholder. Today, some businesses have expanded the concept of those who "invest" in a company from stockholders or shareholders to stakeholders. "Stakeholders are those groups on whom a company depends. They can help the company achieve its goals or stop it dead in its tracks. They include shareholders and members of the financial community, customers, employees, suppliers, communities, and governments. . . . creating value is a matter of taking stakeholders' perspectives into account. . . . For companies with a stakeholder orientation, service to all is the principle reason for being in businesses" (Moss Kanter, 1987, pp. 11-12). Each of the stakeholder constituencies might have different metrics for evaluating the success of a business. At times, some of the measurements seem to conflict. However, evidence is growing that what satisfies employees might also satisfy customers (Peters, 1987) and stockholders. An article in the Wall Street Journal (1997, March 19, B-1) indicated that

> People factors, such as a company's ability to foster employee morale and loyalty and to attract and retain talented people, are drawing scrutiny by investors. . . . Ernst and Young's Center for Business Innovation presented a study of 275 portfolio managers that showed that investor decisions are driven 35% of the time by non-financial factors. A company's ability to attract and retain talented employees ranked fifth among 39 factors that investors used for picking stocks. Only strategy execution, management credibility, quality of strategy and innovativeness ranked higher. The study found that the more non-financial information used, the more they made accurate forecasts on business success.

Several authors and research studies have concluded that one way to satisfy all stakeholders is to focus on satisfying employees. Morris (1996), in an article identifying ways to maximize the return on human capital, wrote that a "satisfied employee can be the catalyst for alignment. . . . employees are the ones who deliver satisfaction to your customers. They are the company's eyes and ears for shifting customer expectations. They are, in effect, the enablers of the company's strategies to deliver value to customers and make the company competitive in its markets" (pp. 15-16). Mendes (1996) cited a study by the Forum Corporation that showed that sixty-five percent of problems in customer service occur because of indifferent or unhelpful employees. According to the study, "only 14 percent of problems were due to a product of poor quality" (p. 10).

In their book, *The Service Profit Chain*, Heskett, Sasser, and Schlesinger (1997) used organizational research to propose a causal model that posited that "there are direct and strong relationships between profit; growth; customer loyalty; customer satisfaction; the value of goods and services delivered to customers; and employee capability, satisfaction, loyalty, and productivity" (p. 11). The theory was based on the proposition that internal service quality drives employee satisfaction which enables the delivery of high value service resulting in customer satisfaction leading to customer loyalty which in turn produces profit and growth (as cited in Hallowell, Schlesinger, & Zornitsky, 1996, p. 22). Ulrich, Halbrook, Meder, Stuchlik, and Thorpe (1991) documented three empirical business case studies on employee and customer attachment. In all cases, they found that "when employees feel an attachment to the firm, they are more likely to share their positive images and feelings about the firm with customers" (p. 90). Their overall observation was that "while job satisfaction may not lead to customer satisfaction directly, service organizations rarely have satisfied customers without having satisfied employees"(p. 28). They also concluded that "employee attitude surveys should be seen as means, not ends. The ultimate end of doing an employee attitude survey is not testing employees, but in making sure that a customer is affected positively by employee attitudes (p. 101). These findings have been supported by studies in other industries. For example, Atkins, Stevenson, Marshall, and Javalgi (1996), in a study of marketing techniques of hospitals, found that "a strong relationship exists between employee satisfaction and patients' perceptions of the quality of their care, measured in terms of their intent to return and to recommend the hospital to others" (p. 15). Kotter and Heskett (1992) studied 207 U.S. companies in 22 industries. They found that financially successful companies focused first on fulfilling customer and employee needs and only secondarily on profits (p. 40).

TRANSFORMATION AND MEASUREMENT OF HUMAN RESOURCES

"Human Resource practices represent the policies, procedures, systems, and activities used to shape, monitor, and direct attention of people within an organization" (Ulrich, 1987, p. 173). People costs are frequently perceived to be the highest expense in operating a business. Recently, the intent to control people costs was an important driver in many cost-cutting and downsizing initiatives. A survey conducted by the Wyatt Company in 1991 found that most restructuring efforts fell short of their economic objectives. In his book, *Costing Human Resources: The financial impact of behavior in organizations,* Cascio (1991) reported that "1) only forty-six percent of the companies said their cuts reduced expenses enough over time, in part because four times out of five, managers ended up replacing some of the very people they had dismissed; 2) fewer than one in three said profits increased as much as expected; and, 3) only twenty-one percent reported satisfactory improvements in shareholders' return on investment" (p. 98).

Because of many failed attempts to deal effectively with human assets, Conner and Ulrich (1993) wrote, "Many companies are discovering a need to reinvent the Human Resource function. What is called for is an HR function that expands its focus beyond its traditional operational and transactional role. To improve its effectiveness and have greater impact, the Human Resource function must understand how to add value in the organization by helping line managers align HR strategies, processes, and practices with business needs" (p. 38). In an article entitled "On the edge of oblivion", Fitz-enz (1996) reported that "most consultants believe that the HR department of the next century will be composed of a few highly skilled, business-oriented internal human asset management consultants" (p. 88). Schuler (1990) suggested that "the Human Resource department is being presented with an opportunity to become a significant player on the management team. This is occurring because the Human Resource function is being transformed into a significant management function. Environmental changes are confronting organizations with people issues of great importance and uncertainty. People issues are thus becoming formulated as significant business issues" (p. 49).

There are some important issues that must be resolved if HR is to transform to a new role within organizations. Ulrich (1992) identified some of the issues as a lack of alignment on Strategic Human Resource Management practices, the need for new competencies for Human Resource professionals, and a need for consistent performance metrics. Another barrier to transforming HR might be reputation. "For longer than anyone can remember, staff departments have been viewed as expense centers, overhead, or necessary evils" (Fitz-enz, 1994, p. 84). Fitz-enz (1996) wrote that "even though HR spends less than 1 percent of the operating budget in most organizations, based on the SHRM/Saratoga Institute Annual HR Financial Reports (1986-1995), many executives view it (HR) as a costly enigma. Management knows it needs many employee-related activities handled efficiently. It knows the key to the future is effective management of human assets. Yet, in many companies, management doesn't see HR doing this in a way that adds value" (p. 85).

With the growing competition today, "organizations cannot afford to support people who are not obviously contributing to the strategic goals of the enterprise" (Fitz-enz, 1995, p. 11). And so, "Quietly but steadily, the corporate cost-cutting knife has descended on the Human Resources department. Once considered essential to the restructuring process and therefore immune to drastic downsizing, HR departments have now been whacked down and reengineered dramatically at 58 percent of large U.S. Corporations. . . . Across all industries, HR departments are being reengineered, their functions either eliminated, automated, or outsourced" (Brenner, 1996, p. 61, as cited in *The Conference Board*, 1996). Suddenly, Human Resource practitioners are finding their traditional role under close scrutiny. Ulrich, Losey, and Lake (1997) posited that "the Human Resources function is at a crossroads . . . it must partner effectively with line management to achieve strategic objectives for the corporation, or else face extinction" (p. 3).

Despite the bleak picture, there are several positive outcomes that might result from the transformation of HR. In 1992, a Towers Perrin worldwide study sponsored by IBM showed that "in the year 2000, HR will be responsive to a highly competitive marketplace and global business structures; closely linked to business strategic plans; [and] focused on quality, customer service, productivity, employee involvement, teamwork and workforce flexibility" (Conner & Ulrich, 1994, p. 39). Ulrich (1997) recommended that in order to accomplish the transformation to new roles, HR will develop many core technologies, including " executive development, recruiting and staffing, training and education, rewards and recognition, performance management, employee relations, labor relations, and diversity" (p. 240). In addition, because of the extensive research, such as that of Huselid (1995), Delaney and Huselid (1996), Becker and Gerhart (1996), Gerhart and Milkovich (1990), Arthur (1994), Ichniowski, Shaw, and Prennushi (1994), and MacDuffie (995), Human Resources might be better able to assess the value of people practices and estimate the impact on organizational performance which will enable HR professionals to become true strategic business partners.

SUMMARY

This literature review revealed that despite the rapid and constant rate of change in business today, people throughout generations have derived satisfaction from meeting similar needs to belong to groups, to feel a sense of accomplishment, to participate in organizational and group processes and decisions, to work cooperatively, to fulfill basic physiologic needs, to grow and develop, and to be recognized and acknowledged. Where these needs are met, employees perceive work more positively. Both the individual and the organization are healthier and, as such, are better able to withstand continuing and inevitable change. Because of this, quite often, both the individual and the organization are able to grow and be more successful, thereby providing "wealth" to all stakeholders. This literature review has suggested that it is the responsibility of both HR and line management, working together as partners, to access and enable employee satisfaction and to ensure that organizations have the capacity to implement business strategies and achieve business success.

CHAPTER 3

Methodology

This historical study used data from both employee attitude surveys and data from financial reports of a Fortune 100 company to investigate the relationship between employee satisfaction and business results.

POPULATION

The Company that provided the data for this study is one of the largest chemical companies in the world. It operates 200 manufacturing and processing facilities in 40 countries worldwide (Company Annual Report, 1996). Table 1 indicates the number of people that were employed by the Company during the period of this study.

Table 1. Number of Company Employees Worldwide (thousands) for Each Year of This Study

1991	1992	1993	1994	1995	1996	Total
133	125	114	107	105	97	521,000

Note. Information was obtained from the 1996 Company Annual Report and 1995 Company Data Book.

SAMPLE

The survey instrument, a questionnaire, was distributed to 64,310 employees, or a subset of the total Company population who were identified as the employees of the chemical side of the Company. The sample for this study consisted of 35,600 employees who responded to four em-

39

ployee satisfaction surveys during the six-year period of this research. The respondents were primarily citizens of the United States. On average, this sample was 88% Caucasian, 73% male, and 74% individuals who had been employed by the Company for 10 years or more. A description of the number of surveys distributed, the numbers of surveys returned, and additional descriptions of the sample are presented in Table 2 below.

Table 2 Survey and Sample Descriptions

Survey Year	Population Size	Surveys Distributed	Surveys Returned	Sample Description		
				Caucasian	Male	Tenure
1991	76,168	8,087 (11%)	5,235 (65%)	88%	76%	77%
1992	70,156	9,753 (14%)	4,918 (50%)	90%	70%	73%
1993/1994	61,839	16,394 (26%)	9,427 (58%)	87%	72%	71%
1995/1996	50,315	30,076 (60%)	16,020 (53%)	88%	74%	77%
Totals	258,478	64,310 (25%)	35,600 (55%)			
Average				88%	73%	74%

Note. Data was reported in Response Analysis® and Questar® Survey Reports. Percentage of surveys distributed represents the percent of the total population. Percentage of surveys returned represents percent of surveys distributed. Tenure refers to percent of employees with a tenure of 10 or more years as employees of the Company.

In order to increase the probability that the opinions expressed in the surveys were representative of all Company employees, a random sample stratified by organization and job category was drawn. Appendix A presents the statistical details of the sampling formula. A subset of this resultant sample was used for this study by isolating results of respondents from business units within the Company. These business units were identified as the core businesses within the 1996 Company Annual Report and varied in size, market and industry focus, and maturity.

RESEARCH DESIGN AND PROCEDURES

This research was designed as a descriptive study using correlational statistics. Therefore, by design, this study focused on associations or the strength of the relationships between employee satisfaction variables and business results. The data collection for this study consisted of two main phases: collection and organization of business unit and corporate employee satisfaction survey data and collection and organization of corporate and business unit financial results.

Employee satisfaction data were generated by four employee satisfaction surveys that were administered within the Company during a six-year period by third party vendors. These four surveys contained questions that varied with regards to content, phraseology, and response format. Thirty employee satisfaction variables were isolated by identifying those survey questions that were identical or that had sought to determine satisfaction levels for similar areas. Each employee satisfaction variable was given an alphabetical code. Appendix B contains a description of these variables, survey questions, and references to the year of the survey and source question number.

In each of the four surveys, employees were directed to respond to survey questions by using a five point Likert-type scale. In the survey summary reports provided by the third party vendors to the Company, responses were identified as unfavorable if respondents indicated that they strongly disagreed or disagreed with statements or that they were very dissatisfied or dissatisfied with conditions highlighted in the questions. Those responses to which the respondents indicated that they neither agreed nor disagreed with the statement or where the respondents indicated that they were neither satisfied nor dissatisfied with the statements were identified as neutral. Questions that were answered by a strongly agree or agree or a very satisfied or satisfied response were identified as favorable. For the purpose of this study, the percentage of respondents who responded favorably to the survey questions were tabulated and used to assess trends and to compare with financial results.

Business unit employee satisfaction variables and a calculated business unit employee satisfaction factor were used in determining relationships with business unit financial metrics. Corporate employee satisfaction variables and a calculated corporate employee satisfaction factor were used in the correlations with corporate financial results. The corporate employee satisfaction data included survey results from the core business units and additional data from other business units and subsidiaries of the Company.

Financial data for this study were collected using the Company's internal and published financial documents, including Company Annual Reports. Following collection of financial data, pairwise Pearson correlations were calculated to relate satisfaction and financial results. Employee satisfaction variables and employee satisfaction factors from both the business units and the corporation were correlated with seven business unit financial metrics and nine corporate financial metrics, respectively. Table 3 below summarizes the correlations that were conducted for this study.

Table 3 Pearson Pairwise Correlations Conducted for This Study

Variable Description	No.	Variable Description	No.
Business Unit Employee Satisfaction Factor	1	Business Unit Financial Metrics	7
Business Unit Employee Satisfaction Variables	30	Business Unit Financial Metrics	7
Business Unit Employee Satisfaction Variables	30	Business Unit Financial Factors	3
Corporate Employee Satisfaction Factor	1	Corporate Financial Metrics	9
Corporate Employee Satisfaction Variables	30	Corporate Financial Metrics	9
Corporate Employee Satisfaction Variables	30	Corporate Financial Factors	3

Note. The numbers indicate the number of variables included in the correlational studies.

INSTRUMENTATION

The questionnaires that were used to collect employee satisfaction data used in this study were developed, distributed, collected, and analyzed by third party vendors in collaboration with various representatives from the Company. Response Analysis® was selected to conduct and analyze the 1991 survey. Surveys conducted in 1992 through 1996 were coordinated by Questar®. The employee satisfaction surveys were distributed by mail to employees in April, 1991; June, 1992; January, 1994; and, May, 1996. Cover letters accompanied the surveys that identified the intent and importance of the surveys, guaranteed the confidentiality of the data, and provided instructions for completing and returning the questionnaire. The four surveys varied in length and in the nature and scope of the questionnaire items. Due to changes in corporate strategies, the surveys also differed in the emphasis on topics and in the analysis and presentation of survey results.

Validity and Reliability. Few historical records were available at the time of this study to assess the validity and reliability of the survey questions. However, in a 1993 Questar® report to the Company (p. 21), the vendor indicated that programs, which were developed by the Questar® Quality Assurance department, were used to scan and flag out-of-range, inconsistent, or questionable data. By following strict control procedures, Questar® guaranteed that the data capture process was accurate and more than 99.9% reliable.

In 1994, a factor analysis was conducted by Questar® that yielded data that was used to assess internal consistency. The factor labels and reliability estimates that were determined by using Cronbach's Alpha for categories of employee satisfaction variables ranged from a high of .877 and a low of .750. The results are included in Appendix C.

STATISTICAL TREATMENT OF DATA

Data from the surveys and financial reports were entered into MYSTAT®. Pearson pairwise correlation coefficients were determined to assess the strength of the relationship for employee satisfaction variables and employee satisfaction factors with the business unit and corporate financial metrics. Graphs were generated to visually depict the relationship between the satisfaction variables and the financial results. Correlation results were ranked to isolate highly positive and highly negative relationships. In addition to the correlations, standard deviations were calculated for the business unit and corporate employee satisfaction variables to assess the variance during the period of the study. The results were ranked to identify those employee satisfaction variables with the highest and the lowest point estimates.

THREATS TO VALIDITY

The historical nature and the correlational design of this study presented several threats to the validity of the research results. These threats can be classified as issues that impacted the collection of the data, interpretation of the data, and researcher error and bias.

As indicated earlier in the study, two vendors were used by the Company to coordinate the employee surveys. Response Analysis® coordinated the 1991 Company Employee Satisfaction Survey. Questar® conducted the studies for the 1992, 1993-1994, and 1995-1996 Company surveys. Though a vendor effect was a possible threat, a review of the processes used to create, distribute, collect, and analyze the data appeared similar. As a historical study, there was no control over the employee satisfaction variables that were selected for the Company employee satisfaction surveys, the actual questions used in the surveys, or the interpretation and presentation of survey results. Therefore, the phrasing of several of the employee satisfaction survey questions selected for this study varied which might have influenced research outcomes.

Retrieving survey data was made difficult due to the reorganization and restructuring that had taken place in the Company during the period of this study. When the changes in structure impacted the business unit, both the employee satisfaction survey results and the financial results were obtained from the originating business unit in an attempt to minimize error. For example, if a business unit was divided into smaller units during the period of the study, both survey data and financial data was drawn from the original business unit.

Results for several of the employee satisfaction variables and financial results were not available in the historical records. Missing data were derived using regression for the following nine variables: 1991 US Earnings, 1991 Shareholder Return on Investment, 1992 survey results for questions related to balance (L) and personal benefits from organizational goals (R), and 1995/1996 survey results for questions related to input to decisions (D), dignity and respect by supervisor (H), job security (Y), pay (BB), and benefits (CC). Imputed data were only used to calculate corporate factors and to correlate the employee satisfaction variables with those factors.

Several inconsistencies were found in the historical financial reports. When these occurred, the most recent results were used in the data collection which were assumed to be the most accurate description of financial status. An additional threat to validity might be due to the timing or distribution of the employee satisfaction surveys. Employee satisfaction surveys were not distributed in alignment with the fiscal year and, therefore, might have influenced correlational outcomes.

Testing bias might have impacted the honesty of the employee responses. For example, employee responses to survey questions might have been influenced either upward or downward by the organizational reaction to previous survey results. Also, as indicated in the description of the sample, respondents to the surveys were primarily citizens of the United States. Both the business unit and Corporate financial data reflected global results. Therefore, the sample used for the employee satisfaction data was only a subset of that which contributed to the financial results.

Finally, though no attempt was made to infer causality between the employee satisfaction and financial variables, validity might have been impacted by a concept described by Borg and Gall (1994) as presentism, or the tendency to interpret past events using concepts and perspectives from current knowledge and experience (p. 825).

CHAPTER 4

Results

The results of this study will be presented in three groups: business unit findings, corporate findings, and variability findings.

BUSINESS UNIT FINDINGS

Correlation of Business Unit Employee Satisfaction Factor with Business Unit Financial Metrics. Thirty employee satisfaction variables were investigated in this study. These variables are listed in Appendix B of this document. The employee satisfaction survey results for these variables that were obtained from business units were reduced to a business unit employee satisfaction factor. This factor was correlated to seven business unit financial metrics, or indicators of business unit success used by the Company.

Table 4 presents the results of this correlation. Shareholder Value Added (SVA) yielded a correlation coefficient of .65, the only result that was significant at the .01 level. The relationships between the employee satisfaction factor and the other business unit financial metrics, including Growth, Return on Net Assets (RONA), After-Tax Operating Income (ATOI), Fixed Cost Productivity, and Controllable Cash Flow produced correlation coefficients ranging from .30 to .46. Sales resulted in the weakest relationship yielding a correlation coefficient of -.04.

Correlation of Business Unit Employee Satisfaction Variables with Business Unit Financial Metrics. Table 5 presents a listing of the

**Table 4 Correlation of Business Unit Employee Satisfaction Factor
with Business Unit Financial Metrics**

Business Unit Financial Metric	Correlation Coefficient
Shareholder Value Added (SVA)	.65**
Growth	.46
Return on Net Assets (RONA)	.37
After-Tax Operating Income (ATOI)	.35
Fixed Cost Productivity	.33
Controllable Cash Flow	.30
Sales	-.04
$N= 16$	

Note. The Employee Satisfaction Factor was derived using means for each
employee satisfaction variable A through DD from each of the Business Units.
** indicates significance at the .01 level.

ten strongest relationships that resulted from correlating the employee
satisfaction variables with the business unit financial metrics. Shareholder Value Added (SVA) resulted in a range of correlation coefficients
from .58 to .70, representing moderately strong relationships with the
business unit employee satisfaction variables.

Shareholder Value Added (SVA) demonstrated the strongest relationships with the following employee satisfaction variables: personal development (V, $r =$ .70), promotion practices (T, $r =$ .68), job satisfaction (P, $r =$
.66), involvement and participation (C, $r =$ .66), use of skills and abilities
(S, $r =$ .64), opportunity to improve skills (U, $r =$ .62), value for diversity (J,
$r =$ .61), fair treatment (I, $r =$ .60), Company ability to compete (O, $r =$ .59),
and creativity and innovation (AA, $r =$ .58). Seven of the ten strongest correlation coefficients that resulted in correlating Growth with the business
unit employee satisfaction variables were significant at the .05 level. One
of the correlation coefficients was significant at the .01 level. The correlation coefficients ranged from .44 to .65. The correlation of employee satisfaction variables with Growth resulted in significant correlation
coefficients with overall satisfaction with the Company (A, $r =$ .65), the
Company's ability to compete (O, $r =$ .62), job security (Y, $r =$ .62), Company change strategies (N, $r =$ .61), balance (L, $r =$ .59), job satisfaction (P,
$r =$ .58), pay (BB, $r =$ .53), and direction of the Company (M, $r =$ .51).

Table 5. Correlation of Business Unit Employee Satisfaction Variables with Business Unit Financial Metrics

Shareholder Value Added	Growth	Return on Net Assets	After-Tax Operating Income	Fixed Cost Productivity	Controllable Cash Flow	Sales
V = .70**	A = .65**	X = .60*	X = .49	O = .60*	C = .46	W = .31
T = .68**	O = .62*	BB = .59*	S = .48	W = .53*	S = .46	BB = .19
P = .66**	Y = .62*	Y = .54*	T = .45	B = .47	Q = .37	Y = .15
C = .66**	N = .61*	P = .52*	V = .44	E = .43	J = .36	X = .13
S = .64*	L = .59*	B = .48	P = .43	K = .42	K = .36	S = .13
U = .62*	P = .58*	R = .46	C = .43	P = .41	P = .35	A = .10
J = .61*	BB = .53*	AA = .46	O = .35	N = .40	DD = .33	J = .09
I = .60*	M = .51*	O = .43	AA = .35	V = .39	I = .33	E = .07
O = .59 *	T = .46	I = .43	K = .35	A = .38	V = .32	D = .05
AA = .58*	B = .44	N = .42	J = .34	X = .35	Z = .30	P = .05

N=16

Note. Table includes the ten strongest positive relationships when correlating Business Unit Employee Satisfaction Variables with Business Unit Financial Metrics. Letters correspond to the employee satisfaction variables identified in survey questions. See Appendix B for descriptions.

* indicates significance at the .05 level.

** indicates significance at the .01 level.

Ranges for the correlation coefficients that resulted when correlating business unit employee satisfaction variables with the remaining business unit financial metrics are as follows: Return on Net Assets (.42 to .60); After-Tax Operating Income (.34 to .49); Fixed Cost Productivity (.35 to .60); Controllable Cash Flow (.30 to .46); and, Sales (.05 to .31). Correlating the employee satisfaction variables with Sales demonstrated the weakest relationships of the seven business unit financial metrics selected for this study. Return on Net Assets (RONA) yielded moderately strong relationship with opportunities for getting a better job (X, r = .60), pay (BB, r = .59), security (Y, r = .54), and job satisfaction (P, r = .52). Fixed Cost Productivity demonstrated a moderately strong relationship with employee satisfaction with the Company's ability to compete (O, r = .60) and training for the job (W, r = .53). Though the strength of the relationship varied, job satisfaction (P) appeared in the list of the strongest correlations with all seven of the business unit financial metrics. Satisfaction with the Company's ability to compete (O), personal development (V), use of skills and abilities (S), value for diversity (J), and opportunities for a better job (X) appeared in Table 5 with at least four of the seven business unit financial metrics. These six employee satisfaction variables account for 28 of the 70 variables, or 40% of those that demonstrated the strongest relationships with the business unit financial metrics.

Correlation of Business Unit Employee Satisfaction Variables with Business Unit Financial Factors. The business unit financial metrics were reduced to three business unit financial factors to investigate if the selection of the financial metrics for this study might have impacted the relational outcomes with the employee satisfaction variables. Business Unit Financial Factor 3 included Sales, Growth, and Shareholder Value Added data. Business Unit Financial Factor 5 included the data from the same business unit financial metrics plus After-Tax Operating Income and Return on Net Assets. Data from all of the business unit financial metrics were used to calculate Business Unit Financial Factor 7. Table 6 presents the findings of the ten strongest correlations of the business unit employee satisfaction variables with the business unit financial factors.

Though the strengths of the relationships between the employee satisfaction variables and the business unit financial factors differed, with correlation coefficients ranging from .38 to .62, nine of the ten employee satisfaction variables that demonstrated the strongest relationships ap-

Table 6. Correlation of Business Unit Employee Satisfaction Variables with Business Unit Financial Factors

Business Unit Financial *Factor 3*	Business Unit Financial *Factor 5*	Business Unit Financial *Factor 7*
P = .62*	X= .58*	P = .53*
A = .57*	P= .57*	X = .51*
V = .56*	S = .51*	S = .51*
X = .55*	T = .51*	C = .50*
S = .54*	V = .49	V = .49
C = .54*	C = .48	T = .48
O = .54*	O = .47	O = .47
T = .54*	A = .45	A = .42
J = .51*	J = .44	J = .41
U = .50*	AA= .43	I = .38

N=16

Note. Table includes the ten strongest positive relationships when correlating the Business Unit Employee Satisfaction Variables with the Business Unit Financial Factors. Factors were produced using the following: Business Unit Financial Factor 3 includes Sales, Growth, Shareholder Value Added; Business Unit Financial Factor 5 includes Sales, Growth, Shareholder Value Added, After-Tax Operating Income, and Return on Net Assets; Business Unit Financial Factor 7 includes Sales, Growth, Shareholder Value Added, After-Tax Operating Income, Return on Net Assets, Fixed Cost Productivity, and Controllable Cash Flow. Letters represent employee satisfaction variables that are described in Appendix B. * indicates significance at the .05 level.

peared in the list of three factors. These employee satisfaction variables included job satisfaction (P), opportunities for a better job (X), use of skills and abilities (S), involvement and participation (C), personal development (V), promotion practices (T), Company ability to compete (O), overall satisfaction with the Company (A), and value for diversity (J). With the exception of opportunities for a better job (X), the relationships, or the correlation coefficients, decreased as business unit financial metrics were added to the factors.

CORPORATE FINDINGS

Correlation of Corporate Employee Satisfaction Factor with Corporate Financial Metrics. Summary reports from the four employee satisfaction surveys that were supplied by the third party vendors included data identified as corporate responses. The corporate responses included all of the results from the business units selected for this study plus additional data from divested businesses, acquired businesses, and subsidiaries. As with the business unit employee satisfaction results, the corporate employee satisfaction results were reduced to a corporate employee satisfaction factor. This factor was correlated with each of nine corporate financial metrics selected for this study. Table 7 presents the findings of these correlations. US earnings, corporate earnings, return on shareholder investment, and dividends per share of common stock demonstrated strong relationships with the corporate employee satisfaction factor, resulting in correlation coefficients of .97, .93, .90, and .87 respectively. The remaining corporate metrics yielded correlation coefficients ranging from .37 to .79.

Correlation of Corporate Employee Satisfaction Variables with Corporate Financial Metrics. Table 8 presents a list of the ten strongest positive relationships that resulted from correlating corporate employee satisfaction variables with corporate financial metrics. The correlation coefficients ranged from .67 to .99, indicating moderate to very strong relationships. US earnings resulted in the strongest relationship with the corporate employee satisfaction variables, with correlation coefficients ranging from .92 to .99. Dignity and respect by the supervisor (H), pay (BB), and value for diversity (J) resulted in a .99 correlation coefficient with US earnings. Ten employee satisfaction variables demonstrated a relatively strong relationship, where r > .70. These employee satisfaction variables account for 94% of those variables listed in Table 8. Personal development (V), involvement and participation (C), use of skills and abilities (S), dignity and respect by the organization (G), and fair treatment (I) appear in the list of the strongest relationships in all nine of the corporate metrics. Recognition (DD), information to do the job (E), promotion practices (T), opportunity for a better job (X), and cooperation and teamwork (K) appear in the list of the strongest relationships of at least seven of the nine corporate metrics.

Table 9 presents the five strongest negative relationships that resulted when correlating corporate employee satisfaction variables with

Table 7. Correlation of Corporate Employee Satisfaction Factor
with Corporate Financial Metrics

Metric	Correlation Coefficient
US Financial Metrics	
US Earnings	.97**
US After-Tax Operating Income	.70
US Sales	.37
Corporate Financial Metrics	
Corporate Earnings	.93**
Shareholder Return on Investment	.90*
Corporate Sales	.72
Stock Metrics	
Dividends per Share of Common Stock	.87*
Year-end Stock Price	.79
Earnings per Share of Common Stock	.74
N=6	

Note. In order to calculate correlation coefficients, the following were imputed
using regression: 1991 US Earnings, 1991 Shareholder Return on Investment,
1992 value for Balance (L), 1992 value for Personal Benefits from Organizational Goals (R), 1995-96 value for Input into Decisions (D), 1995-96 value for
Dignity and Respect by Supervisor (H), 1995-96 value for Security (Y), 1995-
96 value for Pay (BB), and 1995-96 value for Benefits (CC).
 * indicates significance at the .05 level.
 ** indicates significance at the .01 level.

corporate financial metrics. Correlation coefficients range from -.99 to -
.02. Satisfaction with benefits (CC), balance between concern for financial performance and concern for employees (L), input to decisions (D),
corporate change strategies (N), and direction of the Company (M)
demonstrated a moderate to strong negative relationship with at least six
of the nine corporate financial results, with correlation coefficients ranging from -.97 to -.40. Other employee satisfaction variables that demonstrated moderate to strong negative relationships with corporate financial
metrics included satisfaction with job security (Y) and personal benefits

Table 8. Positive Correlations of Corporate Employee Satisfaction Variables with Corporate Financial Metrics

US Sales	US Earnings	US ATOI	Corporate Share	Corporate Earnings	Corporate Return	Earnings Per Share	Dividends Per Share	Year-End Stock Price
Y = .92**	H = .99**	G = .82*	S = .92**	S = .81*	I = .86*	C = .86*	G = .95**	G = .90*
V = .88*	BB = .99**	I = .82*	C = .91*	G = .81*	G = .86*	S = .85*	I = .94**	S = .90*
C = .87*	J = .99**	S = .82*	G = .91*	C = .80	S = .85*	V = .85*	S = .94**	I = .89*
X = .87*	I = .98**	C = .77	I = .89*	I = .80	K = .79	G = .84*	K = .91*	K = .85*
J = .82*	V = .97**	V = .76	V = .89*	V = .79	E = .78	I = .84*	C = .81*	C = .81*
DD = .82*	G = .95**	E = .75	K = .87*	X = .74	C = .76	X = .80	E = .79	V = .78
S = .72	C = .94**	K = .75	X = .86*	E = .74	T = .74	DD = .78	V = .78	E = .77
G = .69	E = .94**	T = .71	DD = .86*	K = .74	V = .74	E = .78	DD = .75	DD = .74
I = .67	S = .93**	X = .69	AA = .78	DD = .72	X = .67	K = .77	Z = .74	X = .73
AA = .67	T = .92**	DD = .68	E = .77	T = .71	DD = .67	T = .74	T = .73	T = .72

N=6

Note. Letters refer to employee satisfaction variables that are described in Appendix B. Table represents the ten most positive relationships that resulted from the correlation of Employee Satisfaction Variables with Corporate Financial Metrics.
* indicates significance at the .05 level.
** indicates significance at the .01 level.

Table 9 Negative Correlations of Corporate Employee Satisfaction Variables with Corporate Financial Metrics

US Sales	US Earnings	US ATOI	Corporate Share	Corporate Earnings	Corporate Return	Earnings Per Share	Dividends Per Share	Year-End Stock Price
Y = .92**	H = .99**	G = .82*	S = .92**	S = .81*	I = .86*	C = .86*	G = .95**	G = .90*
N = -.77	CC = -.99**	N = -.71	N = -.88*	N = -.74	N = -.72	N = -.78	Y = -.85*	N = -.79
R = -.38	D = -.99**	M = -.48	M = -.40	M = -.44	M = -.52	M = -.45	N = -.81*	CC = -.69
M = -.26	Y = -.99**	L = -.44	L = -.33	L = -.32	L = -.50	L = -.30	CC = -.80	D = -.64
Q = -.11	L = -.98**	D = -.29	D = -.10	D = -.22	D = -.38	D = -.24	D = -.62	Y = -.49
H = -.06	R = -.98**	CC = -.25	R = -.02	CC = -.14	CC = -.38	CC = -.12	L = -.56	L = -.48

N=6

Note. Letters refer to employee satisfaction variables that are described in Appendix B. Table includes the five most negative relationships resulting from the correlation of the Employee Satisfaction Variables with the Corporate Financial Metrics.

* indicates significance at the .05 level.

** indicates significance at the .01 level.

from achieving organizational goals (R), appearing in the list of at least three of the nine corporate financial metrics.

Correlation of Corporate Employee Satisfaction Variables with Corporate Financial Factors. The nine corporate financial metrics selected for this study were reduced to three factors. The Corporate Financial Factor was calculated using data from corporate sales, corporate earnings, and return on shareholder investment. US Sales, US earnings, and US ATOI were used to calculate the US Financial Factor. The Stock Factor was calculated using earnings per share of common stock, dividends per share of common stock and year-end stock price. Table 10 presents those employee satisfaction variables that demonstrated the strongest positive relationships with correlation coefficients arbitrarily identified as greater than or equal to .75.

Involvement and participation (C), personal development (V), use of skills and abilities (S), treatment with dignity and respect by the organization (G), fair treatment (I), and cooperation and teamwork (K) demonstrated a strong positive relationship with all three corporate factors. Other factors that demonstrated relatively strong positive relationships included dignity and respect by supervisor (H), information to do the job (E), recognition for doing a good job (DD), and opportunity for a better job (X).

. Table 11 presents a list of those corporate employee satisfaction variables that resulted in the strongest negative relationship with the factors, with correlation coefficients ranging from -.80 to -.29. Though the strength of the relationship differed, the same employee satisfaction variables were negatively related to all three factors: Corporate Financial Factor, the US Financial Factor, and the Stock Factor. These variables included satisfaction with change strategies (N), input to decisions (D), benefits (CC), job security (Y), direction of the company (M), and balance the concern between financial performance and concern for employees (L).

VARIABILITY IN BUSINESS UNIT AND CORPORATE EMPLOYEE SATISFACTION VARIABLES

In addition to investigating the relationships between employee satisfaction and business unit results, this study attempted to determine the variability of employee satisfaction variables between 1991 and 1996. To this end, both the business unit employee satisfaction variables and the corporate employee satisfaction variables were tracked for the six-year

Table 10. Positive Correlations of Corporate Employee Satisfaction Variables with Corporate Financial Factor, US Financial Factor, and Stock Factor

Corporate Financial Factor	US Financial Factor	Stock Factor
S = .89*	C = .90*	S = .90*
I = .89*	V = .89*	G = .90*
G = .89*	X = .86*	I = .89*
K = .84*	S = .85*	K = .85*
C = .80	DD = .84*	C = .81*
V = .78	G = .82*	V = .78
E = .78	I = .81*	E = .77
H = .75	K = .77	DD = .75

N=6

Note. Table includes the strongest positive relationships, where r> .75, when correlating the Corporate Employee Satisfaction Variables with the Corporate Financial Factor, US Financial Factor, and the Stock Factor. The Corporate Financial Factor includes Corporate Sales, Corporate Earnings, and Shareholder Return on Investment. The US Financial Factor includes US Sales, US Earnings, and US After-Tax Operating Income. The Stock Factor includes Earnings per Share, Dividends per Share, and Year-End Stock Price. Letters represent employee satisfaction variables that are described in Appendix B. In order to calculate correlation coefficients, the following were imputed using regression: 1991 US Earnings, 1991 Shareholder Return on Investment, 1992 value for Balance (L), 1992 value for Personal Benefits from Organizational Goals (R), 1995-96 value for Input into Decisions (D), 1995-96 value for Dignity and Respect by Supervisor (H), 1995-96 value for Security (Y), 1995-96 value for Pay (BB), and 1995-96 value for Benefits (CC). * indicates significance at the .05 level.

period of the study. Standard deviations were calculated to assess variability in the employee satisfaction variables. Table 12 presents a list of the business unit and corporate employee satisfaction variables with the highest and the lowest standard deviation point estimates representing the most and the least variability during the period of this research. Eight of ten employee satisfaction variables that demonstrated the most vari-

Table 11 Negative Correlations of Corporate Employee Satisfaction Variables with Corporate Financial Factor, US Financial Factor, and Stock Factor

Corporate Financial Factor	US Financial Factor	Stock Factor
CC = -.80	N = -.84*	CC = -.80
N = -.78	D = -.66	N = -.79
D = -.76	CC = -.66	D = -.75
Y = -.73	Y = -.52	Y = -.74
L = -.54	M = -.35	L = -.54
M = -.48	L = -.29	M = -.47

N=6

Note. Table includes the six strongest negative relationships when correlating the Corporate Employee Satisfaction Variables with the Corporate Financial Factor, US Financial Factor, and the Stock Factor. The Corporate Financial Factor includes Corporate Sales, Corporate Earnings, and Shareholder Return on Investment. The US Financial Factor includes US Sales, US Earnings, and US After-Tax Operating Income. The Stock Factor includes Earnings per Share, Dividends per Share, and Year-End Stock Price. Letters represent employee satisfaction variables that are described in Appendix B. In order to calculate correlation coefficients, the following were imputed using regression: 1991 US Earnings, 1991 Shareholder Return on Investment, 1992 value for Balance (L), 1992 value for Personal Benefits from Organizational Goals (R), 1995-96 value for Input into Decisions (D), 1995-96 value for Dignity and Respect by Supervisor (H), 1995-96 value for Security (Y), 1995-96 value for Pay (BB), and 1995-96 value for Benefits (CC). * indicates significance at the .05 level.

ability, or the highest standard deviations, during the period of the study in both business unit and corporate results included job security (Y), understanding of personal benefits from achieving organizational goals (R), treatment with dignity and respect by the organization (G), overall satisfaction with the Company (A), confidence in the ability of the Company to compete (O), fair treatment (I), balance between concern for financial performance and concern for employees (L), and use of skills and abilities (S). Satisfaction with the direction of the Company (M) and satisfac-

Table 12. Variability in Business Unit and Corporate Employee Satisfaction Variables

Business Results				Corporate Results			
Most Variable		Least Variable		Most Variable		Least Variable	
SD	Mean	SD	Mean	SD	Mean	SD	Mean
Y= 16.35	44.5	X= 4.83	27.6	Y= 26.88	48.9	Z= 4.14	60.5
R= 12.03	45.0	N=4.83	43.6	G= 11.71	54.2	X = 3.92	27.6
G= 11.42	54.0	J= 4.43	49.3	R= 10.35	45.3	K= 3.59	72.6
A= 11.16	51.3	Z= 4.29	59.6	M= 10.08	36.2	E= 3.19	71.8
O= 11.03	52.7	K=4.22	72.5	O= 9.70	51.4	J= 3.13	50.3
I= 9.20	47.0	E= 4.16	71.3	A= 8.96	51.3	P= 2.98	65.4
L= 8.43	23.7	P=4.04	65.3	L = 8.86	23.2	U= 2.97	41.6
S= 8.37	59.8	U=4.01	40.7	I = 8.53	47.4	D= 2.71	29.8
F= 7.60	39.1	H= 3.80	66.7	S= 8.06	61.6	W= 2.09	48.6
Q= 7.02	66.9	D= 3.07	30.2	BB= 7.18	56.6	N= 2.08	48.5

Note. For Business Unit results, $N=16$. For Corporate results, $N=6$. The standard deviation (SD) for the Business Units represents the average SD for business units within the Company. The letters represent employee satisfaction variables that are described in Appendix B. The means represent the mean levels of satisfaction for the period of this study.

tion with pay (BB) demonstrated high variability with corporate employee satisfaction results. Information on the Company (F) and satisfaction with work (Q) demonstrated relatively high variability with the business unit employee satisfaction data.

Nine of ten employee satisfaction variables that resulted in the least point estimates or the lowest standard deviations during the period of the study with both business unit and corporate results included: opportunity for a better job (X), change strategies (N), value for diversity (J), cooperation and teamwork (K), information to do the job (E), job satisfaction (P), opportunity to improve skills (U), input into decisions (D), and employee satisfaction with continuous improvement (Z).

Several factors should be considered when using the data above to develop improvement strategies. In addition to the variability, actual levels of satisfaction should be considered to evaluate effectiveness and assess investments. For example, though both of the following employee satisfaction variables demonstrated low variability during the study, the levels of satisfaction ranged from a low of 27.6 percent favorability for opportunities for a better job (X) to a high of 72.6 percent favorability for cooperation and teamwork (K) which might lead to different improvement strategies.

CHAPTER 5

Conclusions, Discussion, and Recommendations

"In order for a corporation to meet effectively its obligations to share-holders, employees, and society, its top managers must develop a relationship between the organization and employees that will fulfill the continually changing needs of both parties" (Beer et al, 1984, p. 1). In the Company, the employee satisfaction surveys that were conducted during the period of this research were one measure of assessing how well or how poorly the organization performed in meeting employees' needs and expectations. Employees are expected to provide the human resources that are necessary to satisfy all of the other stakeholders of the Company, such as customers and shareholders. Success can be measured in many ways. The financial results that were tracked in this study were one measure of how well or how poorly the Company performed in meeting the needs and expectations of its shareholders.

Authors, such as Cascio (1991), Fitz-enz (1995), and Ulrich (1987), have indicated the critical need for Human Resources to determine and increase their value to their customers, the business units, in economic terms. Past work in utility analysis (Boudreau, 1988) attempted to assign dollar values to selected tasks within Human Resources to help business leaders better understand the costs associated with managing human assets. Though this study was not designed to identify dollar values, it did describe the relationships between employee satisfaction and financial results in descriptive and correlational outcomes so that business and HR leaders might make decisions to invest in Human Resource improvement initiatives that are better aligned with business strategies. Though it was not possible to infer causality between the employee satisfaction and the financial variables, the following conclusions were drawn from the strength of correlational relationships and variances in employee satisfaction variables over time the six year period of this study.

CONCLUSIONS

The strongest relationship that resulted from correlating a Business Unit Employee Satisfaction Factor with Business Unit Financial Metrics was with Shareholder Value Added (SVA), where r = .65. According to Company financial reports, SVA measures the economic profit or value added to the shareholders. The Business Unit Employee Satisfaction Variables that yielded the strongest relationships to SVA were personal development (V), promotion practices (T), job satisfaction (P), involvement and participation (C), use of knowledge and skills (S), opportunity to improve skills (U), value for diversity (J), Company ability to compete (O), fair treatment (I), and creativity and innovation (AA). Correlation coefficients ranged from .58 to .70. These employee satisfaction variables might be representative of the organizational characteristics that employees in the Company value. In 1943, Maslow included many of these employee satisfaction variables in the concept he called "self-actualization" which represented the needs that people have to use their skills, to grow, to develop, and to be recognized in the workplace. Self-actualization has also been described as the desire to become more and more of what one is, to become everything that one is capable of becoming (as cited in Lawler, 1994, p. 30). Maslow noted that motivation based on self-actualization and individual growth needs does not decrease as the needs become satisfied. He argued that as people experience growth and self-actualization, they simply want more. This suggests that employees might need to be continually challenged and might never be totally satisfied with growth opportunities. Though the results of this study suggest that providing growth opportunities for individuals might enhance the capacity for organizational and financial growth, it is not possible to conclude that increasing individual satisfaction with elements of self-actualization at work will automatically and directly increase shareholder value. Several authors and researchers, including Argyris (1993) and Huselid (1995), have cautioned that companies that are doing financially well might simply be better able to invest in satisfying the self-actualization needs of employees which accounts for the strong correlation between employee satisfaction and financial variables.

Several of the employee satisfaction variables that demonstrated a moderate to strong relationship with the financial variables were related to the job itself (P), the ability to use one's skills and ability on the job (S), the need to be recognized for those skills and abilities (DD), and the opportunities to improve job skills (U). Ludeman (1989) described these characteristics as an employee's need for self-fulfillment and directly linked them to a person's search for worth or value in one's job. Hackman and Oldham (1980) did extensive research on employees' need for fulfillment and meaning as related to satisfaction with the job itself. Their research suggested that to motivate workers, managers might seek out ways to make the work more interesting and less routine; recognize work that is well done; allow employees autonomy in the performance of their tasks; and promote those who perform well. In other words, the job should be restructured so that it becomes more meaningful, more challenging, and more intrinsically rewarding to the workers. In both the business unit and Company correlational results of this study, employees expressed a relatively high level of job satisfaction (P), resulting in an average of 65% favorability. Throughout the period of this study, levels of job satisfaction (P) varied only slightly, yielding standard deviations of 4.04 for corporate results. Despite intense organizational change within the Company resulting from such events as changes in executive leadership, business restructuring, and downsizing (Company Annual Reports, 1991–1996), employees remained satisfied with their jobs. By investigating the elements that positively impacted job satisfaction, leaders in the Company might gather additional data to support the use of work design as a business strategy and to increase both job challenge and satisfaction for employees, even during periods of organizational change.

In their book, *Grow to Be Great*, Gertz and Baptista (1995) wrote about the importance of growth to the longevity and sustainability of businesses. They indicated that growth is perceived by most senior executives as the solution to most of their long-term concerns (p. 3). In their research, these authors found that in interviews of chief executives from 180 U.S.-based companies and 100 European-based companies, 94 percent considered growth a top priority. In this study, Growth, or the percentage of increase in sales compared to the previous year, exhibited a moderately strong relationship with overall satisfaction (A), job security (Y), Company ability to compete (O), Company change strategies (N), balance between concern for employees and financial performance (L), job satisfaction (P), pay (BB), and direction of the Company (M). Correlation coefficients which resulted from comparing Growth with these employee satisfaction variables ranged from .51 to .65. The list of variables suggests that employees might have a long term focus and therefore need to understand the direction of the Company. Similar to the relationships observed with correlations to SVA, the data seem to suggest that opportunities for organizational success and growth might be closely linked to employees' need for individual success and growth. This potential relationship presents business leaders with both a problem and an opportunity. Because of the rate of change in large organizations, it is no longer possible to provide the long-term guarantees for employment and opportunities for advancement that were offered in the past (Csoka, 1996). The changes in organizational commitment to employees might be increasing the need for employees to understand business direction so that they can make choices to align and re-align with organizations, inside or external to the Company, in order to take advantage of the greatest perceived opportunities for growth and security. This might result in undesired increases in employee turnover and associated increases in related costs. In this study, employee satisfaction with both the direction of the Company (M) and Company change strategies (N) were negatively correlated with the corporate financial metrics. Correlation coefficients ranged from −.88 to −.26. These results suggest that leaders in the Company might need to seek new ways to communicate and position information about the Company, to develop new relationships or partnerships with employees, to redefine the value of employee contributions, and to reshape ways to share in financial rewards so that both business leaders and employees assume mutual responsibility for business success.

The strength of the relationship of business unit growth to overall satisfaction (A), where r = .65, might represent a summation of the impact of HR practices that were implemented in the Company during the period of this study. In his research in the automobile industry, MacDuffie (1995) recommended that research on HR practices consider "bundles" versus isolating the effect of single HR practices. Cappelli and Singh (1992) observed the importance of organizational "fit" or the adoption of practices into the organizational culture. Overall satisfaction levels might be an indicator of employee perception of the fit of several HR practices in the Company. The overall level of satisfaction might also be an indicator that employees realize that a work environment, like life itself, has positive and negative aspects. Authors Wright and Smye (1996) had indicated that many employees in the workplace had learned to accept a culture of some sacrifice. They wrote that "initially, it is easy to be seduced by the challenge of sacrifice....After all, we're well paid and the more we do for the company, the more we'll share in its success" (p. 80). However, if individuals do not satisfy basic security and safety needs, or perceive equality in the distribution of rewards, or realize personal gain from company success, they may begin to question the purpose for individual sacrifice and seek greater balance between private and professional lives which would create some new challenges for business leaders. In this study, both employee satisfaction with balance (L) and perceiving personal benefits from achieving organizational goals (R) were negatively related to financial results in the Company which might indicate that employees are beginning to question the value and rewards for personal sacrifice.

Much research has been conducted to understand the economic motivation of employees. In this study, employee satisfaction with pay demonstrated a .53 correlation coefficient with Growth and a .99 correlation coefficient with US earnings. Herzberg et al (1957) classified pay as a dissatisfier indicating that motivation does not necessarily result from its improvement. Rather, dissatisfaction increases as a result of deterioration. The strengths of the relationships between the compensation and financial variables in this study might be a reflection of the current economic conditions. Employee perceptions of pay might reflect an aspect of security and survival or might represent a need for status or recognition. Social status and recognition needs might have increased in the Company as other opportunities for recognition, such as promotion and advancement, decreased over time. In many companies, employee focus on pay has led to activities to increase the variety of pay options or compensation plans, including opportunities for gainsharing, or permitting employees to share in the profits of the organization (Lawler, 1981). Within many companies, the intent of the compensation or pay programs is to increase an employee's understanding of how performance relates to pay and to articulate how individual performance adds value to and improves organizational results. If compensation strategies are successful, employees might not only improve their financial situation but also increase their sense of worth and consequently their levels of confidence, self-esteem, and satisfaction (Ludeman, 1989).

Compensation encompasses not only pay, but also benefits, recognition, and other characteristics of the work environment that employees might consider as recompense for their work (Wilson, 1995). In this study, employee satisfaction with benefits received by the Company (CC) demonstrated negative relationships with corporate financial results. Correlation coefficients ranged from -.80 to -.12. In the long term, the perception of the sacrifice of benefits for organizational success might impact employee loyalty and commitment to achieving organizational goals, which eventually might impact ability to execute business strategies (Reichheld, 1996). Employee satisfaction with recognition (DD) was strongly correlated with eight of the nine corporate financial metrics, with correlation coefficients ranging from .67 to .86. This suggests that employees view pay, benefits, and recognition differently. As indicated earlier in this study, 77% of the sample had been with the Company for over 10 years. During the period of this research, employee satisfaction with security (Y) resulted in the highest point estimates, indicating that security was the most changed of the thirty employee satisfaction variables studied. During the period of this study, the employee population of the Company had been decreased by 36,000, or approximately 27%. Security issues had not only become a threat to employees, but the data from the study indicated that security (Y) was negatively correlated to the corporate, US, and stock factors with correlation coefficients ranging from -.74 to -.52. According to Maslow (1943), the lack of security threatens the lowest levels of human needs. It generates fear and, as such, blocks opportunities for both individual growth and self-actualization. Wright and Smye (1996, p. 40) wrote:

> Fear is a powerful emotion, yielding anxiety, self-protection, and re-
> sentment....Working under a siege mentality, employees are trans-
> formed into a sullen and unmotivated workforce. Demoralized
> individuals shift into a survival mode, producing just what is de-
> manded of them and no more. At a time when management is strug-
> gling to restructure and boost productivity, employees are least capable
> of contributing.

These authors also noted that insecurity might impact creativity and innovation. "Nothing disturbs the peace of creative minds as much as fear....People who have to protect themselves in abusive corporate cultures have little time or mental energy for inspiration" (Wright & Smye, 1996, p. 183). In this study, satisfaction with creativity and innovation (AA) was moderately related with Shareholder Value Added (r = .51). Ironically, the more turbulent the business environment, the more organizations need to provide security and encourage employees to take risks in order to foster creativity and innovation and to provide for growth and increased shareholder value.

According to Lawler (1994, p. 22), "People want to be treated fairly. They observe what happens to other people and if they receive either 'too much' or 'too little' in comparison to other people it makes them uncomfortable". Satisfaction with the treatment of employees, which in this study included a perception of fairness (I), receiving dignity and respect from both the supervisor (H) and the organization (G), and value for diversity (J) was strongly and positively correlated with corporate financial factors. When compared to corporate financial metrics, correlation coefficients for these employee satisfaction variables ranged from .67 to .99. Research conducted by Locke (1969) suggested that a person's level of satisfaction with perceptions of fairness and equity is a function both of how much they receive and of how much they feel they should and want to receive (as cited in Lawler, 1994, p. 85). Argyris (1993, p. 30) noted that "the organization, as a subsociety, may influence (1) what the individual will tend to desire, (2), the probability of achieving it, and (3) the meaning of the success or failure". Frequently, the perception of fairness is influenced by the interaction of the employee with the supervisor. Lawler (1994) noted that, whereas this relationship is significant in impacting individual performance, during times of organizational change, employees might have an increased need to perceive fairness by the organization. If both the relationships with the supervisor and the organization are satisfactory, employees might be able to deal more effectively with change and might be less distracted by issues related to the work environment.

Several authors and researchers, including McLagan and Nel (1995), Kravetz (1988), Huselid (1995), and Lawler (1992), have identified that firms that engaged in participative practices have increased levels of employee satisfaction and significantly outperformed companies that did not use such practices. Within the Company, the level of employee satisfaction with involvement and participation (C) was strongly correlated with all of the corporate financial metrics chosen for this study. Correlation coefficients ranged from .76 to .94. However, the level of employee satisfaction with involvement and participation (C) was only 46% favorable. The strength of the relationships and relatively low level of satisfaction suggest that leaders in the Company might benefit from implementing strategies to increase levels of employee involvement and participation. Because the concept of participation was not well defined by the questions used in the employee satisfaction surveys, additional qualitative research might be necessary in the Company to clarify employee definitions of involvement and participation and to identify employee expectations.

Employee satisfaction with cooperation and teamwork (K) was strongly correlated with seven of the nine corporate financial metrics targeted in this research. Correlation coefficients ranged from .74 to .91.

These findings support the concept that employees' desires to satisfy social needs are related to business success. Likert (1961) commented that "to have a friendly supportive relationship day in and day out with one's colleagues is more important to most people than relatively minor financial rewards" (p. 15). Business leaders might experience some interesting challenges fulfilling employee social needs as workforces become more global, diverse, and transient, and as work environments become more flexible, electronic, and "virtual".

DISCUSSION

Generalizability. Results from this study were determined by using specific Company data, from a specific set of business units, within a specific point of time, and subjected to a specific set of organizational circumstances. Therefore, though many large organizations experienced similar changes during the period of this study, the findings are not generalizable either to business units currently within the Company or to organizations external to the Company. However, this study provided baseline data with which could be used to continue research on employee satisfaction trends and relationships between employee satisfaction and financial variables and to assess similarities and differences between business units and other companies.

Implications of the Study. "Organizations increasingly conduct attitude surveys to determine their employees' feelings of satisfaction, to understand how the organization operates, and to determine the effects of particular management practices and organization designs....Research on job satisfaction remains important, both because of the insights it provides into quality-of-work-life issues, and because of its impact on organizational effectiveness" (Lawler, 1994, pp. xiv-xvi).

This study demonstrated that despite the numerous variables that can impact financial results and the complexities and dynamics between human and organizational behaviors, it is possible to differentiate the strengths of relationships between employee satisfaction variables and financial metrics. However, relational data alone is insufficient for enhancing decisions to invest in Human Resource improvement initiatives. Trends, or the degree to which employee satisfaction increases or decreases over time, benchmarks, or the comparison of employee satisfaction results to industry trends or organizational goals and objectives, and organizational investments, or the past commitment of resources to improve satisfaction levels, must also be considered when deciding to invest in Human Resource improvement initiatives.

This study modeled only one way to align information about people with information about profits. By providing a framework, the results might influence future research designs and impact the design of future employee satisfaction studies within the Company.

RECOMMENDATIONS FOR FUTURE RESEARCH

Because of the inability to infer causality by the correlational design of this study, future research designs might benefit from incorporating the study of lag phases to provide additional insights on the relationship between employee satisfaction and financial variables. Schuster (1986) posited that there might be a lag of one to three years between implementing improvement initiatives and realizing organizational results (p. 157). Results from lag phase studies might provide additional insight on the relationship between variables, aid decision-making and long-term planning, and provide organizational metrics for evaluating improvement initiatives, i.e., reducing the cycle time of actualizing results from initiatives. Due to the volatility of business units, extending the studies over longer periods of time might also provide additional insights on the relationships of employee satisfaction to rates of organizational growth and business survival.

Jac Fitz-enz, founder of the Saratoga Institute which produces an annual Human Resource Effectiveness Report, claimed that "sixty to seventy percent of those in the HR field aren't using any method to measure their effectiveness and those that are sometimes are measuring the wrong things" (Thornburg, 1992, p. 67). Fitz-enz posited that hard data would give the HR professional proof of program worth or, conversely, ammunition to illustrate what programs are not working and should be dropped or changed. It is important that future data on employee attitudes not only be collected but, as in this study, be analyzed based on the support of and alignment with business outcomes. In his book, *Human Resource Champions,* Ulrich (1997) maintained that HR can do more to help organizations meet business challenges and suggested that HR rethink the nature of their contributions to the organization. He recommended that HR develop a better understanding of where the function fits in the organization's overall strategy, demonstrate ways it can create value, and show how it can help the organization respond to competitive pressures. To increase organizational value, future studies might employ the concept of the balanced scorecard (Kaplan & Norton, 1996) to investigate the interrelationships and correlations between levels of satisfaction of all organizational stakeholders, i.e., customers, employees, shareholders, and society.

If organizations plan to hold leaders more accountable for managing the human assets of the Company, then employee attitude surveys might be useful in evaluating the effectiveness of organizational leaders. Willingham (1997) observed that effective leaders had a fundamental belief that he called the "People Principle," which stated that "all people have unlimited potential that has been largely unrecognized and untapped. When discovered and accessed, this potential can lead them [employees] to far greater levels of productivity than they ever imagined, causing them to feel better about themselves and enjoy life more" (p. 12). If people are the key to a sustained competitive advantage (Pfeffer, 1994), then leadership performance should include an assessment of how well human assets are managed for both short- and long-term business success. In their book, *Leveraging People and Profit*, authors Nagle and Pascarella (1998) suggested that leaders in the future be "altrupreneurs" which they defined as those who conduct the affairs of an enterprise with conspicuous regard for the welfare of others (p. 11). A change in leadership evaluation may necessitate discarding some of the old paradigms and models about successful leaders or, at the very least, enlarge the concept of a good leader as one who cares about people and profits. Future studies might investigate different aspects of the impact of leadership on employee satisfaction. Examples might include the investigation of the impact of executive compensation on employee perception of the health of work environments or the use of employee satisfaction as a measure of the success of leadership development initiatives. Finally, as companies become more global and as survey data from worldwide employees becomes more available, there are opportunities for future studies to compare the intercultural similarities and differences in levels of employee needs and levels of satisfaction and consequent impact on firm performance.

SUMMARY

Employees "wants" are best summarized by the author Max DePree (1989, p. 23) who wrote:

> What is it that most of us want from work? We would like to find the
> most effective, most productive, most rewarding way of working to-

gether....We would like a work process and relationships that meet our personal needs for belonging, for contributing, for meaningful work, for the opportunity to make a commitment, for the opportunity to grow and be at least reasonably in control of our own destinies. Finally, we'd like someone to say "Thank you".

The outcomes of this study indicated that within the Company, personal development (V), involvement and participation (C), use of employee skills and abilities (S), promotion practices (T), and opportunities for a better job (X) were most positively and strongly correlated to both business unit and corporate financial results. In the 1950s, Herzberg and his associates observed that employees were motivated by factors such as achievement, recognition, responsibility, growth, and advancement. Almost 50 years later, this study demonstrated that those characteristics are the employee satisfaction variables that are most strongly related to financial success of a business. The outcomes of this study support empirically what many people know intuitively. The interpretation and value of this research is dependent on individual philosophies and future research regarding the causal relationships among work related attitudes, work motivation, job performance, and organizational results. If future research should indicate that work conditions influence employee attitudes, which in turn influence employee effort and performance, which impacts organizational performance, then this study provided leaders in the Company with data on where to focus and invest efforts in improving the work environment that might be better aligned with enhancing financial results. If future research should indicate that employee attitudes are the consequence and not the determinant of motivation and performance, then the results of this study helped leaders in the Company identify which employee satisfaction variables might be most impacted by organizational success. If, as some believe, the variables that influence individual attitudes and organizational success are too numerous and dynamic and the recursivity between variables too complex, then this study provided a description of how changes within the Company influenced the relationship between employee satisfaction and financial results during a designated time in the Company's history.

In Ecclesiastes, Chapter 3, verse 22, it is written "There is nothing better than for a man to rejoice in his work" (*Womens' Devotional Bible, p.729*). The correlational outcomes of this study suggest that there might be nothing better for the Company than to rejoice in employees who rejoice in their work.

References

Adams, J. S. (1963). Toward an understanding of inequity. *Journal of Abnormal Psychology, 67,* 422-436.

Allee, V. (1997). *The knowledge evolution.* Boston: Butterworth-Heinemann.

Argyris, C. (1995). *Integrating the individual and the organization.* New Brunswick, New Jersey: Transaction Publishers.

Argyris, C. (1993). *Knowledge for action.* San Francisco, California: Jossey-Bass.

Arnold, H. J., & Feldman, D. C. (1982). A multivariate analysis of the determinants of job turnover. *Journal of Applied Psychology, 67,* 350-360.

Arnold, D. G. (1951). *Attitude toward authority and sociometric status as factors in productivity and job satisfaction.* Unpublished dissertation, Los Angeles, California: University of California.

Arthur, J. B. (1994). Effects of human resource systems on manufacturing performance and turnover. *Academy of Management Journal, 37,* 670-687.

Atkins, P., Stevenson, Marshall, & Javalgi, R. G. (1996, Winter). Happy employees lead to loyal patients. *Journal of Health Care Marketing,* 15-23.

Baird, L., & Meshoulam, I. (1988). Managing two fits of strategic human resource management. *Academy of Management Review, 13,* 116-128.

Bartel, A. P. (1994). Productivity gains from the implementation of employee training programs. *Industrial Relations, 33,* 411-445.

Bass, B. M. (1985). *Leadership and performance beyond expectations.* New York, New York: Free Press.

Bateman, T. D., & Strasser S. (1984). A longitudinal analysis of the antecedents of organizational commitment. *Academy of Management Journal, 27,* 95-112.

Becker, B., & Gerhart, B. (1996). The impact of human resource management on organizational performance: Progress and prospects. *Academy of Management Journal, 39*(4), 779-801.

Becker, T. E., Billings, R. S., Eveleth, D. M., & Gilbert Nichole. (1996). Foci and bases of employee commitment: Implications for job performance. *Academy of Management Journal, 39*(2), 464-482.

Beer, M., Spector, B., Lawrence, P., Mills, D., & Walton, R. E. (1984). *Managing human assets.* New York, New York: The Free Press.

Begin, J. P. (1991). *Strategic employment policy: An organizational systems perspective.* Englewood Cliffs, New Jersey: Prentice-Hall.

Berlet, K. R., & Cravens, D. M. (1991). *Performance pay as a competitive weapon: A compensation policy model for the 1990s.* New York, New York: John Wiley & Sons, Inc.

Best, F. (1973). *The future of work.* Englewood Cliffs, New Jersey: Prentice-Hall.

Birchard, P. (1995, March). Failure's four friends. *Supervision, 6*-9.

Bishop, J. (1994). The impact of previous training on productivity and wages. In L. Lynch (Ed.), *Training and the private sector: International comparisons,* 161-199. Chicago, Illinois: Chicago University Press.

Black, S. E., & Lynch, L. M. (1996, May). Human-capital investments and productivity. *AEA Papers and Proceedings, 86*(2), 263-267.

Blanchard, K., & Johnson, S. (1983). *The one minute manager.* New York, New York: Berkley Books.

Bluedorn, A. C. (1979). Structure, environment, and satisfaction: Toward a causal model of turnover from military organizations. *Journal of Military and Political Sociology, 7,* 181-207.

Bluedorn, A. (1982). A unified model of turnover from organizations. *Human Relations, 35,* 135-153.

Bookbinder, S. M. (1996). The employee perspective. In B. Hackett (Ed.), *The new deal in employee relationships (pp.* 12-17). New York, New York: The Conference Board, Inc.

Borg, Walter R. & Gall, Meredith D. (1989). White Plains, New York; Longman.

Borman, W. C. (1991). Job behavior, performance, and effectiveness. In M. D. Dunnette & L. M. Hough (Eds.), *Handbook of Industrial and Organizational Psychology (second edition),* 271-326. Palo Alto, California: Consulting Psychologists Press.

Boudreau, J. W. (1988). Utility analysis; A new perspective on human resource management decision making. In L. Dyer (Ed.), *Human Resource Management Evolving roles and responsibilities,* 125-186. Washington, D. C.: Bureau of National Affairs.

Brenner, L. (1996). The disappearing HR department. *CFO, March,* 61-64.

Bridges, W. (1980). *Job Shift.* Reading, Massachusetts: Addison-Wesley.

Brooking, A. (1997). *Intellectual capital.* New York, New York: International Thompson Business Press.

Canfield, J., & Miller, J. (1996). *Heart at work.* New York, New York: McGraw-Hill.

Cappelli, P., & Singh, H. (1992). Integrating strategic human resources and strategic management. In D. Lewin & O. S. S. Mitchell, P. (Eds.), *Research frontiers in industrial relations and human resources.* Madison, WI: Industrial Relations Research Association.

Carnevale, D. G. (1996, Summer). The human capital challenge in government. *Review of Public Personnel Administration,* 5-13.

Cascio, W. F. (1991). *Costing Human Resources: The financial impact of behavior in organizations.* Boston, Massachusetts: PWS-KENT Publishing Company.

Cascio, W. F. (1993). Downsizing: What do we know? What have we learned? *Academy of Management Executive, 7*(1), 95-104.

Caudron, S. (1994). HR leaders brainstorm the profession's future. *Personnel Journal, 73*(8), 54-62.

Clampitt, P. G., & Downs, C. W. (1993). Employee perceptions of the relationship between communication and productivity: A field study. *Journal of Business Communications, 30*(1), 5-28.

Clegg, C. W. (1983). Psychology of employee lateness, absence, and turnover: A methodological critique and an empirical study. *Journal of Applied Psychology, 68,* 88-101.

Coch, L., & French, J. (1948). Overcoming resistance to change. *Human Relations, 1,* 512-352.

Cohen, W. A., & Cohen, N. (1993). *The paranoid corporation.* New York, New York: American Management Association.

Conference Board (1993). *Closing the performance gap.* New York: The Conference Board.

Conference Board (1996). *The new deal in employment relationships.* New York: The Conference Board.

Conner, J., & Ulrich, D. (1993). Human Resource roles: Creating value, not rhetoric. *Human Resource Planning,* 38-49.

Cooper, M., Morgan, B., Foley, P. M., & Kaplan, L. B. (1979, January-February). Changing employee values: Deepening discontent? *Harvard Business Review,* 117-125.

Cotton, J. L., & Tuttle, J. (1986). Employee turnover: A meta-analysis and review with implications for research. *Academy of Management Review, 11,* 55-70.

Cotton, J. L., Vollrath, D. A., Froggatt, K. L., Lengnick-Hall, M. L., & Jennings, K. R. (1988). Employee participation: Diverse forms and different outcomes. *Academy of Management Review, 13*(1), 8-22.

Csoka, L. (1996). In B. Hackett (Ed.), *The new deal in employee relationships.* New York, New York: The Conference Board, Inc.

Cutcher-Gershenfeld, J. (1991). The impact on economic performance of a transformation in industrial relations. *Industrial and Labor Relations Review, 44,* 241-260.

Davis, K. (1977). *Human behavior at work.* New York: McGraw-Hill.

DeGeus, A. (1997). *The living company.* Boston, Massachusetts: Harvard Business School Press.

Deiner, E., Emmons, R., Larsen, R. J., & Griffin, S. (1985). The satisfaction with life scale. *Journal of Personality Assessment, 49,* 71-75.

Delaney, J. T., & Huselid, M. A. (1996). The impact of Human Resource management practices on perceptions of organizational performance. *Academy of Management Journal, 39*(4), 949-969.

Denton, K. D. (1991, September-October). What's wrong with these employees? *Business Horizons,* 45-49.

DePree, M. (1989). *Leadership is an art.* New York, New York: Bantam Doubleday Dell Publishing Group, Inc.

Dewey, B. J., & Hawk, E. J. (1996, May-June). Economic value: A better approach to people management. *Compensation & Benefits Review, 30-36.*

Dougherty, T. W. Bluedorn, A.C., & Keon, T. L. (1985). Precursors of employee turnover: A multi-sample causal analysis. *Journal of Organizational Behavior, 6,* 259-271.

Downs, C. W., & Hazen, M. D. (1977). A factor analytic study of communication satisfaction. *Journal of Business Communication, 14*(3), 63-73.

Drucker, P. F. (1974). *Management.* New York, New York: Harper & Row.

Drucker, P. F. (1989). *The new realities.* New York: Harper & Row.

Etzioni, A. (1964). *A comparative analysis of complex organizations.* New York: Free Press.

Farkas, A., J., & Tetrick, L., E. (1989). A three-wave longitudinal analysis of the causal ordering of satisfaction and commitment on turnover decisions. *Journal of Applied Psychology, 74*(6), 855-868.

Finance Department of the Company. (1996). *Financial Metric Definitions: 1996 Business Unit Reporting.*

Fitz-enz, J. (1994, February). HR's new score card. *Personnel Journal,* 84-91.

Fitz-enz, J. (1995). *How to measure human resources management.* New York, New York: McGraw-Hill, Inc.

Fitz-enz, J. (1996, May). On the edge of oblivion. *HRMagazine,* 85-88.

Fitz-enz, J. (1997). *The 8 practices of exceptional companies.* New York, New York: American Management Association.

Galbraith, C., & Merrill, G. B. (1991). The effect of compensation program and structure on SBU competitive strategy. *Strategic Management Journal, 12,* 353-370.

Gallup, G. (1988, August). Employee research: From nice to know to need to know. *Personnel Journal,* 42-43.

Garner, R. (1996, June). There are best places to work and there are successful companies. Is there a connection? *Computerworld,* 58-63.

Gerhart, B., & Milkovich, G. T. (1990). Organizational differences in managerial differences and managerial compensation and firm performance. *Academy of Management Journal, 33,* 663-691.

Gertz, D. L., & Baptista, J. (1995). *Grow to be great.* New York, New York: The Free Press.

Glisson, C., & Durick, M. (1988). Predictors of job-satisfaction and organizational commitment in human service organizations. *Administrative Quarterly, 33,* 61-81.

Gomez-Mejia, L. (1992). Structure and process of diversification, compensation strategy, and firm performance. *Strategic Management Journal, 13,* 381-397.

Gordon, E. E. (1997, January/ February). Investing in Human Capital: The case for measuring training ROI. *Corporate University Review,* 41-42.

Griffin, R. W. (1983). Objective and social sources of information in task redesign: A field experiment. *Administrative Science Quarterly, 28,* 184-200.

Griffin, R. W. (1991). Effects of work redesign on employee perceptions, attitudes, and behaviors: A long-term investigation. *Academy of Management Journal, 34*(2), 425-435.

Gruenberg, M. (1979). *Understanding job satisfaction.* New York: JohnWiley & Sons.

Hackman, J. R., & Oldham, G. (1980). *Work redesign.* Reading, Massachusetts: Addison-Wesley.

Hackman, J. R., & Oldham, G. R. (1975). Development of the Job Diagnostic Survey. *Journal of Applied Psychology, 60,* 159-170.

Hallowell, R., Schlesinger, L. A., & Zornitsky, J. (1996). Internal service quality, customer and job satisfaction: Linkages and implications for management. *Human Resource Planning,* 20-31.

Hambrick, D., & Snow, C. (1989). Strategic reward Systems. In C. Snow (Ed.), *Strategy, Organization Design, and Human Resources Management.* Greenwich, CT: JAI Press.

Henkoff, R. (1993). Companies that train best. In *Fortune, March, 1993, 62.* New York, New York: The Conference Board, Inc.

Herzberg, F., Mausner, B., Peterson, R., & Capwell, D. (1957). *Job attitudes: Review of research and opinion.* Pittsburgh, Pennsylvania: Psychological Service of Pittsburgh.

Heskett, J. L., Sasser, E., & Schlesinger, L. (1997). *The service profit chain.* New York, New York: The Free Press.

Hollenbeck, J., & Williams, C. R. (1986). Turnover functionally versus turnover frequency; A note on work attitudes and organizational effectiveness. *Journal of Applied Psychology, 71,* 606–611.

Hoppock, R. (1935). *Job satisfaction.* New York: Harper.

Howard, J. L., & Frink, D. D. (1996). The effects of organizational restructure on employee satisfaction. *Group & Organization Management, 21*(3), 278–303.

Hulin, C. I., & Smith, P. C. (1964). Sex differences in job satisfaction. *Journal of Applied Psychology, 48,* 88–92.

Hulin, C. L., Roznowski, M., & Hachiya, D. (1986). Alternative opportunities and withdrawal decisions. *Psychological Bulletin, 97,* 233–250.

Hull, R. L., & Kolstad, A. (1942). Morale on the job. In G. Watson (Ed.), *Civilian morale.* Boston, Massachusetts: Houghton Mifflin.

Hunter, J. E., Schmidt, F. L., & Jackson, G. B. (1982). *Meta-analysis: Cumulating research findings across studies.* Beverly Hills, California: SAGE Publications.

Hurst, D. K. (1995). *Crisis & renewal.* Boston, Massachusetts: Harvard Business School Press.

Huselid, M. A. (1995). The impact of Human Resource Management practices on turnover, productivity and corporate financial performance. *Academy of Management Journal, 38* (3), 635–672.

Huselid, M. A. & Becker, B. E. (1996). Methodological Issues in Cross-sectional and panel estimates of the Human Resource-firm performance link. *Industrial Relations, 35* (3), 400–422.

Ichniowski, C., Shaw, K., & Prennushi, G. (1993). *The effects of Human Resource Management practices on productivity.* Unpublished manuscript, Carnegie Mellon University.

Ichniowski, C., & Shaw, K. (1995). Old dogs and new tricks: Determinants of the adoption of productivity-enhancing work practices. *Brookings Papers on Economic Activity,* 1–65.

Ichniowski, C., Kochan, T. A., Levine, D., Olson, C., & Strauss, G. (1996). What works at work: Overview and assessment. *Industrial Relations, 35*(3), 299–333.

International Survey Research (1996, July). Global happiness ratings. *Management Review,* 53.

Jaffe, D. T., Scott, C. D., & Tobe, G., R. (1994). *Rekindling commitment.* San Francisco, California: Jossey-Bass.

Johansen, R., & Swigart, R. (1994). *Upsizing the individual in the downsized organization.* Reading, MA: Addison-Wesley.

Jones, G. R., & Wright, P. M. (1992). An economic approach to conceptualizing the utility of Human Resource practices. In G. R. Ferris (Ed.), *Research in Personnel and Human Resources, Volume 10.* Greenwich, Connecticut: JAI Press.

Jones, M. (1996, July) Four trends to reckon with. *HR Focus, 22-23.*

Judge, T. A., & Watanabe, S. (1993). Another look at job satisfaction-life satisfaction. *Journal of Applied Psychology, Volume 78,* (6), 939-948.

Kacmar, M. K., & Ferris, G. R. (1989). Theoretical and methodological considerations in the age-job satisfaction relationship. *Journal of Applied Psychology, 74* (2), 201-207.

Kaplan, R. S., & Norton, D. P. (1996). *The balanced scorecard.* Boston, Massachusetts: Harvard Business School Press.

Katz, H. C., Kochan, T. A., & Gobeille, K. R. (1983). Industrial relations performance, economic performance and QWL programs: An interplant analysis. *Industrial and Labor Relations Review,* (37), 3-17).

Katz, H., Kochan, T. A., & Keefe, J. (1988). Industrial Relations and Productivity in the U.S. Automobile Industry. *Brookings Paper on Economic Activity, 3,* 685-715.

Katz, H., Kochan, T. A., & Weber, M. (1985). Assessing the effects of Industrial relations and quality of working life on organizational performance. *Academy of Management Journal, 28*(3), 509-527.

Katz, R. (1978). Job longevity as a situational factor in job satisfaction. *Administrative Science Quarterly, 23,* 204-223.

Katzell, R. A. (1964). Personal values, job satisfaction, and job behavior. In H. Borrow (Ed.), *Man in a world of work.* Boston: Houghton Mifflin.

Kayser, T. A. (1994). *Building team power.* New York, New York: Irwin Professional Publishing.

Kerr, J. (1985). Diversification strategies and managerial rewards: An empirical study. *Academy of Management Journal, 28,* 155-179.

Klaas, B. S., & McClendon, J. A. (1996). To lead, lag, or match: Estimating the financial impact of pay level policies. *Personnel Psychology, 49,* 121-141.

Kotter, John & Heskett, James (1992). Corporate culture and performance. New York; The Free Press.

Kouzes, J. M., & Posner, B. Z. (1988). *The leadership challenge.* San Francisco, California: Jossey-Bass.

Kravetz, D. (1988). *The Human Resources Revolution.* San Francisco, California: Jossey-Bass.

Labovitz, G., & Rosansky, V. (1997). *The power of alignment.* New York, New York: John Wiley & Sons, Inc.

Lakewood Report Briefs. (1996). Investing in people. *The Lakewood Report Briefs, 2*(11), 12.

Lance, C. E. (1991). Evaluation of a structural model relating job satisfaction, organizational commitment, and precursors to voluntary turnover. *Multivariate Behavioral Research, 26,* 137-162.

Lawler, E. I. (1990). *Strategic pay: Aligning organizational strategies and pay systems.* San Francisco, California: Jossey-Bass.

Lawler, E. (1981). *Pay and organization development.* Reading, Massachusetts: Addison-Wesley.

Lawler, E. (1992). *The ultimate advantage: Creating the high-involvement organization.* San Francisco, California: Jossey-Bass.

Lawler, E. E. (1994). *Motivation in work organizations.* San Francisco, California: Jossey-Bass.

Lengnick-Hall, C., & Lengnick-Hall, M. L. (1988). Strategic human resource management: A review of the literature and a proposed typology. *Academy of Management Review, 13,* 454-470. .

Levering, R. (1988). *A great place to work.* New York, New York: Avon Books.

Likert, R. (1967). *The human organization.* New York: McGraw-Hill.

Likert, R. (1961). *Patterns of management.* New York: McGraw-Hill.

Locke, E. A. (1968). What is job satisfaction. *American Psychological Association Convention Proceedings,* September. San Francisco, California.

Locke, E. A. (1969). What is job satisfaction? *Organizational Behavior & Human Performance, 4,* 309-336.

Locke, E. A. (1976). The nature and causes of job satisfaction. In M. D. Dunnette (Ed.), *Handbook of Industrial/Organizational Psychology* (1297-1349). Chicago: Rand McNally.

Locke, E., & Schweiger, D. M. (1979). Participation in decision making: One more look. In B.M. Staw (Ed.), *Research in Organizational Behavior, 1,* 265-339.

Ludeman, K. (1989). *The worth ethic.* New York, New York: E. P. Dutton.

Maccoby, M. (1995). *Why work?.* Alexandria, Virginia: Miles River Press.

MacDuffie, J. P. (1995). Human resource bundles and manufacturing performance: Organizational logic and flexible production systems in the world auto industry. *Industrial and Labor Relations Review, 48*(2), 197-221.

Marsh, R., & Mannari, H. (1977). Organizational commitment and turnover; A prediction study. *Administration Science Quarterly, 22,* 57-75.

Maslow, A. H. (1943). A theory of human motivation. *Psychological Review, 50,* 370-396.

Mathieu, J. E., & Zajac, D. M. (1990). A review and meta-analysis of the antecedents, correlates, and consequences of organizational commitment. *Psychological Bulletin, 108,* 171-194.

McClelland, D. (1987). *Human motivation.* New York: Cambridge University Press.

McClusky, H., & Strayer, F. J. (1940). Reactions of teachers to the teaching situation. *School Review, 48,* 612-623.

McCoy, T. J. (1992). *Compensation and motivation.* New York, New York: American Management Association.

McEvoy, G. M., & Cascio, W. F. (1989). Cumulative evidence of the relationship between employee age and job performance. *Journal of Applied Psychology, 74*(1), 11-17.

McEvoy, G. M., & Cascio, W. F. (1987). Do good or poor performers leave? A meta-analysis of the relationship between performance and turnover. *Academy of Management Journal, 30*(4), 744-762.

McGregor, D. (1960). *The human side of enterprise.* New York: McGraw-Hill.

McLagan, P., & Nel, C. (1995). *The age of participation.* San Francisco, California: Berrett-Koehler Publishers, Inc.

McNeese-Smith, D. (1996). Increasing employee productivity, job satisfaction, and organizational commitment. *Hospital and Health Services Administration, 41*(2), 160-175.

Mendes, A. (1996). *Inspiring commitment.* Chicago, Illinois: Irwin Professional Publishing.

Meyer & Allen (1991). A three component conceptualization of organizational commitment. *Human Resource Management Review, 1,* 61-89.

Miles, R., & Snow, C. (1984, Summer). Designing strategic human resource systems. *Organizational Dynamics,* 36-52.

Miller, K., & Monge, P. (1986). Participation, satisfaction, and productivity: A meta-analytic review. *Academy of Management Journal, 29,* 727-753.

Milligan, Patricia (1996). In B. Hackett (Ed.), *The new deal in employment relationships.* New York, New York: The Conference Board, Inc.

Mills, C. W. (1951). The meanings of work throughout history. In F. Best (Ed.), *The future of work.* Englewood Cliffs, New Jersey: Prentice-Hall.

Mindell, M. G., & Gorden, W. I. (1981). *Employee values in a changing society.* New York, New York: American Management Association.

Mohrman, S. A., Lawler, E. E., & Ledford, G. E. (1996, January-February). Do employee involvement and TQM programs work? *Journal for quality and participation,* 6-10.

Morris, T. (1996, December-January). Employee satisfaction: Maximizing the return on human capital. *CMA Magazine,* 15-17.

Moss Kanter, R. (1987, December). A management Christmas carol. *Management Review,* 11-13.

Mottaz, C. J. (1987, August). Age and work satisfaction. *Work & Occupations, 14*(3), 387-409.

Mowday, R. T., Porter, I. W., & Steers, R. M. (1982). *Employee-organization linkages: The psychology of commitment, absenteeism, and turnover.* San Diego, CA: Academic Press.

Mowday, R. T., Steers, R. M., & Porter, L. W. (1979). The measurement of organizational commitment. *Journal of Vocational Behavior, 14,* 224-247.

Nagle, Bernard A., & Pascarella, Perry (1998). *Leveraging people and profit; The hard work of soft management.* Boston: Butterworth-Heinemann.

Napier, N., & Smith, M. (1987). Product diversification performance criteria and compensation at the corporate manager level. *Strategic Management Journal, 18,* 195-201.

Neil, C. C., & Snizek, W. E. (1988). Gender as a moderator of job satisfaction. *Work and Occupations, 15*(2), 201-219.

Nelson, B. (1996, July). Dump the cash, load on the praise. *Personnel Journal,* 65-70.

Niehoff, B. P., Enz, C. A., & Grover, R. A. (1990). The impact of top-management actions on employee attitudes and perceptions. *Group & Organizational Studies, 15*(3), 337-352.

Noer, D. (1995). *Healing the wounds.* San Francisco, California: Jossey-Bass.

Opren, C. (1979). The effects of job enrichment on employee satisfaction, motivation, and performance: A field experiment. *Human Relations, 189-217.*

Ostroff, C. (1992). The relationship between satisfaction, attitudes, and performance: An organizational level analysis. *Journal of Applied Psychology, 77*(6), 963-974.

Ouchi, W. G. (1981). *Theory Z.* New York: Avon.

Peters, T. J., & Waterman, R. H. J. (1982). *In search of excellence.* New York, New York: Warner Books.

Peters, T. (1987). *Thriving on chaos.* New York, New York: Alfred A. Knopf, Inc.

Pfeffer, J. (1994). *Competitive advantage through people.* Boston, Massachusetts: Harvard Business School Press.

Phillips, J. J. (1996). *Accountability in human resource management.* Houston, Texas: Gulf Publishing Company.

Pinchot, G., & Pinchot, E. (1996). *The intelligent organization.* San Francisco, California: Berrett-Koehler Publishing Company.

Pitts, R. A. (1976). Diversification strategies and organizational policies of large diversified firms. *Journal of Economics and Business, 8,* 181-188.

Pond, S. B., & Geyer, P. D. (1987). Employee age as a moderator of the relation between perceived work alternatives and job satisfaction. *Journal of Applied Psychology, 72*(4), 552-557.

Porter, L. W. (1961). A study of perceived need satisfactions in bottom and middle management jobs. *Journal of Applied Psychology, 45,* 1-10.

Priority Management Systems. (1990). *The 21st century workplace: An international survey about working in a time of transition.* Vancouver, Canada: Priority Management Systems, Inc.

Quinn, R. P., Staines, G., & McCollough. (1974). *Job satisfaction: Is there a trend?.* Washington, D.C.: U.S. Department of Labor.

Rain, J. S., Lane, I. M., & Steiner, D. D. (1991). A current look at the job satisfaction/ life satisfaction relationship; Review and future considerations. *Human Relations, 44,* 287-307.

Rappaport, A. (1978). Executive incentives versus corporate growth. *Harvard Business Review, 56*(4), 81-88.

Reichheld, F. F. (1996). *The loyalty effect.* Boston, Massachusetts: Harvard Business School Press.

Rhodes, S. R. (1983). Age-related differences in work attitudes and behavior: A review and conceptual analysis. *Psychological Bulletin, 93,* 328-367.

Rice, R., Near, J. P., & Hunt, R. G. (1980). The job satisfaction/life satisfaction relationship: A review of empirical research. *Basic and Applied Social Psychology, I,* 37-64.

Rogers, J. D., Clow, K. E., & Kash, T. J. (1994). Increasing job satisfaction of service personnel. *Journal of Services Marketing, 8*(1), 14-26.

Rosen, R. H. (1991). *The healthy company.* Los Angeles, California: Jeremy P. Tharcher, Inc.

Sauser, W. I. J., & York, C. M. (1978). Sex differences in job satisfaction: A reexamination. *Personnel Psychology, 31,* 537-547.

Savery, L. K. (1996). The congruence between the importance of job satisfaction and the perceived level of achievement. *Journal of Management Development, 15*(6), 18-28.

Schaffer, R. H. (1953). Job satisfaction as related to need satisfaction in work. *Psychological Monographs, Number 364, 67*(14).

Schiemann, W. A. (1983). Major trends in employee attitudes toward compensation. In Schiemann (Ed.), *Managing Human Resources.* Princeton, New Jersey: Opinion Research Corporation.

Schmitt, N., & Mellon, P. (1980). Life and job satisfaction: Is the job central? *Journal of Vocational Behavior, 16,* 51-58.

Schneider, B., Ashworth, S. D., Higgs, C. A., & Carr, L. (1996). Design, validity, and use of strategically focused employee attitude surveys. *Personnel Psychology, 49,* 695–705.

Schneider, B., & Bowen, D. E. (1985). Employee and customer perceptions of service in banks: Replication and extension. *Journal of Applied Psychology, 70,* 423–433.

Schneier, R. (1997, March–April). People Value Add: The new performance measure. *Strategy & Leadership,* 14-19.

Schuler, R. S. (1990). Repositioning the Human Resource function: Transformation or demise? *Academy of Management Executive, 4*(3), 49-60.

Schuster, F. E. (1986). *The Schuster Report.* New York, New York: John Wiley & Sons, Inc.

Senge, P. M. (1990). *The fifth discipline.* New York, New York: Doubleday/ Currency.

Shonhiwa, S. O., & Gilmore, H. L. (1996, Winter). Development of Human Resources: A portfolio strategy. *SAM Advanced Management Journal,* 16–23.

Shull, G. R. (1995, January). The survey fix. *Training,* 138.

Sisson. (1969). *Sisson's synonyms.* West Nyack, New York: Parker Publishing Company.

Slater, M. (1973). Tailor incentive compensation to strategy. *Harvard Business Review, 51*(2), 94–102.

Snetsinger, D., & Pellet, G. (1996, July-August). Making employee research pay off. *CMA Magazine,* 13–15.

Soujanen, W. W., McDonald, M. J., & Swallow, G. L., and Soujanen, W. W. (1975). *Perspectives on job enrichment and productivity.* Atlanta, Georgia: Publishing Services Division, School of Business Administration, Georgia State University.

Steagall, Jeffrey W., & Hale, Robert L. (1994). *MYSTAT® for Windows®.* Cambridge, MA: Course Technology, Incorporated.

Stewart, T. A. (1997). *Intellectual capital.* New York, New York: Doubleday/ Currency.

Sveiby, K. E. (1997). *The new organizational wealth.* San Francisco, California: Berrett-Koehler Publishers, Inc.

Swanson, R., & Holton, E. F. (1997). *Human Resource Development: Research Handbook.* San Francisco, California: Berrett-Koehler Publishers.

Syedian, H. (1995, May). The rewards of recognition. *Management Today,* 72–74.

Taber, T. D. (1991). Triangulating job attitudes with interpretive and positivist measurement methods. *Personnel Psychology, 44,* 577-600.

Tait, M., Padgett, M. Y., & Baldwin, T. T. (1989). Job and life satisfaction: A reevaluation of the strength of the relationship and gender effects as a function of the date of the study. *Journal of Applied Psychology, 74*(3), 502-507.

Terpstra, D. E., & Rozell, E. J. (1993). The relationship of staffing practices to organizational level measures of performance. *Personnel Psychology, 46,* 27-48.

Tett, R. P., & Meyer, J. P. (1993). Job satisfaction, organizational commitment, turnover intention, and turnover: Path analyses based on meta-analytic findings. *Personnel Psychology, 46,* 259-293.

Thompson, C., Kopelman, R. E., & Schrieshiem, C. A. (1992). Putting all one's eggs in the same basket: A comparison of commitment and satisfaction among self-and organizationally employed men. *Journal of Applied Psychology, 77,* 738-743.

Thornburg, L. (1992). The white knight of HR effectiveness. *HRMagazine, November,* 67-69.

Thurbin, P. (1995). *Leveraging knowledge.* London, England: Pitman Publishing.

Thurstone, L., & Chave, E. (1929). *The measurement of attitude.* Chicago: University of Chicago Press.

Tomasko, R. M. (1996). *Go for growth.* New York, New York: John Wiley & Sons, Inc.

Turner, N., & Lawrence, P. R. (1965). *Industrial jobs and the worker.* Boston, Massachusetts: Harvard Graduate School of Business Administration.

U. S. Department of Labor Monograph. (1974). Job Satisfaction: Is there a Trend? Volume 30, 4-5.

U.S. Department of Labor. (1993). *High performance work practices and firm performance.* Washington, D. C.: Government Printing Office.

Ulrich, D. (1987). Organizational capability as a competitive advantage: Human Resource professionals as strategic partners. *Human Resource Planning, 10*(4), 169-183.

Ulrich, D. (1992). Strategic and Human Resource planning: Linking Customers and Employees. *Human Resource Planning, 15*(2), 47-62.

Ulrich, D. (1997). *Human Resource champions.* Boston: Harvard Business School Press.

Ulrich, D. (1998, January-February). A New Mandate for Human Resources. *Harvard Business Review, 76*(1), 124-134.

Ulrich, D., Halbrook, R., Meder, D., Stuchlik, M., & Thorpe, S. (1991). Employee and customer attachment: Synergies for competitive advantage. *Human Resource Planning, 14*(2), 89-103.

Ulrich, D., Losey, M., & Lake, G. (1997). *Tomorrow's HR management.* New York: John Wiley & Sons.

Ulrich, D., & Lake, D. (1990). *Organizational capability.* New York, New York: John Wiley & Sons, Inc.

Vandenberg, R. J., & Lance, C. E. (1992). Examining the causal order of job satisfaction and organizational commitment. *Journal of Management, 18*(1), 153-167.

Vroom, V. H. (1964). *Work and motivation.* New York, New York: John Wiley & Sons.

Wagner, J. A. I. (1994). Participation's effects on performance and satisfaction: A reconsideration of research evidence. *19, 2,* 312-330.

Wagner, J. A., & Gooding, R. Z. (1987). Shared influence and organizational behavior: A meta-analysis of situational variables expected to moderate participation-outcome relationships. *Academy of Management Journal, 30*(3), 524-541.

Ward, E. A., & Davis, E. (1995, Summer). The effect of benefit satisfaction on organizational commitment. *Compensation and Benefits Management,* 35-40.

Weber, C., & Rynes, S. L. (1991). Effects of compensation strategy on pay decisions. *Academy of Management Journal, 34,* 86-109.

Williams, L. J., & Hazer, J. T. (1986). Antecedents and consequences of satisfaction and commitment in turnover models: A reanalysis using latent variable structural equation methods. *Journal of Applied Psychology, 71,* 219-231.

Willingham, R. (1997). *The people principle.* New York, New York: St. Martin's Press.

Wilson, T. B. (1995). *Innovative reward systems for the changing workplace.* New York, New York: McGraw-Hill.

Womack, J. P., & Jones, D. T. (1996). *Lean thinking.* New York, New York: Simon & Schuster.

Women's devotional bible. (1995). Grand Rapids, MI: Zondervan Press.

Woodward, H., & Buchholz, S. (1987). *Aftershock.* New York, New York: John Wiley & Sons, Inc.

Wright, L. &. Smye., M. (1996). *Corporate abuse.* New York, New York: Macmillan.

Wright, P. M., & McMahan, G. C. (1992). Theoretical perspectives for Strategic Human Resource Management. *Journal of Management, 18*(2), 295-320.

Yukl, G. (1994). *Leadership in organizations.* Englewood Cliffs, New Jersey: Prentice-Hall, Inc.

Zigarelli, M. (1996). Human Resources and the bottom line. *Academy of Management Executive, 10*(2), 63-64.

Zimney, S. A. (1994). *Job commitment: Employer concern and worker loyalty.* Cambridge, Massachusetts: Cambridge Reports/ Research International.

Zoltners, A. A., Sinha, P. K., & Murphy, S. J. (1997). *The fat firm.* New York, New York: McGraw-Hill.

Appendix A

SAMPLING FORMULA

The following is the sampling formula used to randomly stratify the sample for this study. The formula appeared in a survey sample selection report prepared for the Mayflower Group, a consortium of benchmark companies, on April 10, 1984.

$$n = \frac{N \, Z^2 \, (PQ)}{N \, T^2 + Z^2 \, (PQ)}$$

where:

    n = number of respondents necessary.

    P = proportion responding favorably to the question—assumption is P= .50.

    T = tolerance for error represents + or - error around p value.

    Z = z score at .95 confidence level (1.96).

    N = population size.

    Q = proportion responding negatively.

Appendix B

Variable	VariableName/ Question Nume	Survey Question
A	Overall Satisfaction 91-1, 92-52, 94-86, 96-61	Considering everything, how would you rate your overall satisfaction in the Company at the present time?
B	Company Comparison 91-11, 92-50, 94-90, 96-60	How do you rate the Company as a company to work for compared to other companies?
C	Involvement/Participation 91-3, 92-41, 94-78, 96-27	How satisfied are you with your involvement in decisions that affect your work?
D	Input to Decisions 91-16F, 92-12, 94-14, **	Sufficient effort is made to get the opinions and thinking of people who work here.
E	Information to do Job 91-16A, 92-17, 94-2, 96-10	I have enough information to do my job well.
F	Information on the Company 91-7, 9-45, 94—81, 96-16	How satisfied are you with the information you receive from management on what's going on in the Company?
G	Dignity & Respect by Organization 91-17F, 92-29, 94-29, 96-34	I am treated with dignity and respect by the organization.
H	Dignity & Respect by Supervisor 91-18A, 92-23, 94-54, **	I am treated with dignity and respect by my immediate supervisor.
I	Fair Treatment 91-17D, 92-21, 94-30, 96-37	I am treated fairly by the organization.
J	Value for Diversity 91-37G, 92-28, 94-45, 96-46	How do you rate the Company/leadership/work location on the value for diversity?
K	Cooperation/ Teamwork 91-16T, 92-18, 94-7, 96-25	The people I work with cooperate to get the job done.

Variable	VariableName/ Question Nume	Survey Question
L	Balance 91-30, **, 94-18, 96-20	In the Company, the need for financial performance is balanced with concern for employees.
M	Direction of the Company 91-16GG, 92-2, 94-19, 96-11	Leadership in this organization gives me a clear picture of the direction in which the Company is headed.
N	Change Strategies 91-16K, 92-13, 94-17, 96-18	The Company is making the changes necessary to compete effectively.
O	Company Ability to Compete 91-17H, 92-22, 94-43, 96-19	How do you rate your organization on its ability to compete with other companies?
P	Job Satisfaction 91-2, 92-51, 94-84, 96-59	Considering everything, how satisfied are you with your job?
Q	Satisfaction with Work (Job) 91-16P, 92-10, 94-3, 96-26	My work gives me a feeling of personal accomplishment.
R	Personal Benefits from Organizational Goals 91-16CC, **, 94-5, 96-54	It is clear to me how I will personally benefit if I help my organization meet its goals.
S	Use of Skills and Abilities 91-16N, 92-14, 94-10, 96-23	My job makes good use of my skills and abilities.
T	Promotion Practices 91-17N, 92-39, 94-38, 96-45	How do you rate the Company on pro-moting well-qualified people?
U	Opportunity to Improve Skills 91-16M, 92-8, 94-9, 96-42	I am given a real opportunity to improve my skills in this Company.
V	Personal Development 91-37J, 92-35, 94-47, 96-29	How satisfied are you with development, i.e., offering opportunities and encour-agement to employees to fully develop and use their strengths and values?
W	Training for Job 91-9, 92-44, 94-80, 96-43	How satisfied are you with the training you receive for your present job?
X	Opportunity for Better Job 91-5, 92-42, 94-79, 96-44	How satisfied are you with your opportu-nity to get a better job in this company?
Y	Job Security 91-12, 92-38, 94-23, **	How do you rate the Company in provid-ing job security for people like yourself?

Variable	VariableName/ Question Nume	Survey Question
Z	Continuous Improvement 91-16U, 92-1, 94-8, 96-24	I feel encouraged to come up with new and better ways of doing things.
AA	Creativity and Innovation 91-37I, 92-34, 94-46, 96-55	People at my work location are encouraged (encouraged and rewarded) to be creative and innovative.
BB	Pay 91-13, 92-27, 94-21, **	How do you rate the amount of pay you get on your job?
CC	Benefits 91-14, 92-33, 94-24, **	How do you rate your total benefits program (insurance, medical, etc.)?
DD	Recognition 91-4, 92-47, 94-83, 96-58	How satisfied are you with the recognition you receive for doing a good job?

Note. Survey questions are referenced by year of the survey followed by the question number. "**" indicates that no question was identified that was similar in content or phraseology for that year of the survey.

Appendix C

1994 Survey: Factor Labels and Internal Consistency Reliability Estimates (Alpha)

Factor	Label	Alpha
1	Employee Respect	.877
2	Job Identification	.746
3	Communication from Management	.917
4	Immediate Supervisor	.910
5	Organizational Commitment	.895
6	Job Satisfaction	.876
7	Working Conditions	.730
8	Competitiveness	.866
9	Rewards and Recognition	.887
10	Work Environment	.750

Note. Values documented in Questar® 1994 report to the Company.

Index

For Product Safety Concerns and Information please contact our EU
representative GPSR@taylorandfrancis.com
Taylor & Francis Verlag GmbH, Kaufingerstraße 24, 80331 München, Germany

www.ingramcontent.com/pod-product-compliance
Ingram Content Group UK Ltd.
Pitfield, Milton Keynes, MK11 3LW, UK
UKHW021632240425
457818UK00018BA/368